R.E.I. Editions

All of our ebooks can be read on the following devices:
- Computer
- eReaders
- iOS
- android
- Blackberries
- windows
- Tablet
- Cellular

Daphne & Chloé

Australian Flowers

ISBN: 978-2-37297-1676

Daphne & Chloé

Australian Flowers

R.E.I. Editions

Book Index

Australian Flowers

Australian Bush Flower Essences are to today 69 plus 19 Essences create from the combination Of Flowers Australians And I am States introduced from Ian White, biologist And psychologist Australian. Not I am still very known And used by the general public, but are highly appreciated by Floritherapists and we find Australian Flowers included in many herbal and homeopathic complexes. They are among the most powerful flowers and widely used after Bach flowers, they have a lot of energy elevated, a of the more high between the remedies floral. The aborigines Australians they have always used the Flowers for deal with emotional distress or imbalance, as it occurred in the ancient Egypt, in India, Asia And South America. Use of the Essences Floral has known a long tradition until to become very popular in medieval Europe. Be Hildegard Von Bingen (12th century AD) and Paracelsus (15th century) they left testimony written of habit common Of collect flower dew to deal with some ailments from the ball emotional. Ian White, last Of five generationsOf psychologists And biologists Therapists that they have always used natural remedies, is the discoverer and developer of the Essences ofFlowers Australians. Ian is grown up in the "Bush" (expression Australian used for to define a part wild of the territory). There Grandmother Of Ian, expert in use of the plant Australians, she used to take her nephew with her for walks in the "Bush", how did with there mother Of Ian. Through there her deep experience And knowledge, has could indicate to him the numerous beneficial properties of plants and flowers. Thank you, Ian he developed a deep respect for nature, which served him well to become a pioneer and operator engaged in the research of quality more rare And rebalancing of the plant of the continent Australian. It is a pristine continent, loaded with ancient power. Currently, Australia is knowing a moment of new and pervading energetic vitality which, combined with the innate potential regenerative from the Land, does of Australian Essences of unique remedies.

Australian flowers exist in trade in essences concentrate from 15 ml.

- For prepare a blend yes they pour seven drops Of each of the essences of the stock bottle choices , in a 30 ml bottle with dropper; a quarter is added Of brandy (serves alone how preservative And can   to be replaced by apple cider vinegar by increasing the dose) and 3/4 of water mineral natural.

Yup recommend not insert more Of 4 or 5 remedies for turn.

The dose, both for adults both for children, consists of seven drops to be taken twice a day (morning and evening) under the tongue, or in a little water. Essences should be hired for about winds days or a month, exception done for essences particularly powerful. Being a treatment of the everything natural And deprive Of toxicity, not present none contraindication, not they cause effects collateral, can be combined without problems with both traditional medicines and a homeopathic ones (of which they are considered complementary) or ad other flower remedies. Blends of were also produced Ready-made Australian flowers designed to address specific states emotional. We remember However that there flower therapy not is symptomatological, so not is said that these compositions have an effect on all people equally because everyone person is different give her other And, for example, one state Of "anxiety" Of two people different, also self yes exhibition with there itself symptoms, probably not is caused give it same imbalance emotional. For this is important get to advise the compositions personal Of essences floral suitable specifically to each of us.

Australian Bush Flowers are prepared with a method similar to that of the other floral repertoires, ie placing the flower corollas in a full glass bowl of water Of source and exposing them to the Sun for some hours. For some flowers there Preparation follows mode a bit' different, For example, the exposure nocturnal at the light lunar.

The content he comes then filtered And diluted with a even amount of brandy. From this "mother essence" is obtained then the so-called "concentrate" or stock bottle, placing some 7 drops in a flask from 15 ml. containing 2/3 of brandy And 1/3 of water pure.

How it happens for the flowers Of Bach, also the essences floral Australian women should be chosen based on the observation of emotions andof the moods of the moment, which are a source of greater suffering for the person. Once you have identified the flowers with which compose the mixture, pour 7 drops of the remedy or remedies chosen in a 30 ml. dropper bottle, filled with water mineral natural And two teaspoons Of brandy how preservative.

- The standard dosage of Australian Bush Flowers Essences is Of seven drops from to hire orally morning And evening. Yup can   prepare a alone remedy (there which action Sara At that time particularly "targeted", deep and fast), or mix between They remedies different.

In this case And advisable not exceed 4 or 5 essences and, if possible, try to choose flowers give her property between They kindred And synergistic for to deal a specific problem. Australian flowers are also very effective inskin application and can be added to creams, gels, oils for the massage, medicated ointments or diluted in water bath. For a treatment topical there quantity recommended is Of about 7 drops Of each remedy choice, from amalgamate in half cup Of cream; in the basin from bath they go, instead , pay 15–20 drops Of Everything is fine essence. There duration of the treatment depends always from reply individual.

A positive reaction is often obtained in about two weeks and on average two months are sufficient to rebalance many problematic psychophysical. Some flowers particularly "powerful" (how, for example, Waratah) they exercise Of usual very fast action, even in a few days. Many times after having resolved an inner discomfort or conflict, they can emerge other emotional imbalances, which will gradually be treated with flowers matching.

Not exists danger Of reactions allergic or effects collateral, therefore the remedies Australians can be administered quietly to children, Senior citizens orsick people.

In rare cases, a slight swelling may occur at the beginning of the therapy accentuation of the symptoms, but this reaction initial it goes considered how a signal Of "unlock" energetic And generally of short term.

Alpine Mint Bush

Useful for give new force at people that they perform a service, dealing with other people for whom they are responsible (those who carry out assistance jobs in which they give their all, be physically be emotionally, And they risk Of run out). Revitalize infusing a new joy And a renewed enthusiasm in that what are they doing.
Very useful also for the people that they assist a familiar, staying available twenty four hours to the day, for example, in the case of a child with handicaps or invalid, of the partner that it becomes quadriplegic or paraplegic or Of a relative elderly affection from the disease Of Alzheimers. The weight Of a responsibility Of such proportions leads to a lot of effort, both physically and mentally, with the danger Of a exhaustion.
Ideal for therapists who are in daily contact with both physical and emotional problems of people and have the need Of to remain always very concentrate And intuitive having to make decisions that will affect the lives of other. Very appropriate for those who play a role that it involves of the choices that they will affect the Welfare or there condition of the other, making, however, possible a Certain degree Of impartiality And detachment for protect the own self. It could be useful for social workers, hospital workers and others all people that they cover roles of great responsibility.

- Essence works on a mental and emotional level first that yes verify one state Of exhaustion physicist. It restores people's vitality, bringing a renewed enthusiasm, joy And momentum respect to the They task.

The remedy can be used effectively in a preventative manner, but is not indicated for the end-of-day exhaustion of nature purely physical, in which other essences such as Banksia are useful Rob, Macrocarpa, Old Man banksia.

- The essence renew the enthusiasm, there joy And there compassion for that is that we are living.

When there joy And the taste from the life yes I am completely turned off by an excess of empathy, responsibility and concern for someone else. For idealistic people who have chosen a caring job, but are now dubious e disillusioned because they see that in the work not nothing changes.

In the maternity, for there tiredness or the exhaustion mental or emotional that comes from paying constant attention to the baby.

Angelsword

Angelsword is able to restore the general energy that surrounds the auric field by eliminating negativity.

It is a very powerful essence to be used even after undergoing anesthesia due to surgery, episodes of loss of consciousness, after taking drugs or after violent trauma or physical shock. Confusion And misunderstanding due to influences negative external. Loss of capacity of the Truth and of Faith.

Rediscovered of the values of the past. Renewed communication withthe own The. Useful in case Of problematic food promoting clear communication with the higher self and the discernment to objectively see and be aware ofthat is that is actually happening.

To cleanse the aura. It allows you to find your own truth by sifting through the information, teachings or messages channeled, for recognize what is possibly right for themselves. This essence is for those who doubt spiritual truths and are confused. The essence works by enabling the individual to succeed see the personal and transpersonal past as a photograph.

- It does not cure the past, but it allows access to it.

The function of Angelsword has there quality Of offer protection from influences external. Before Of to work with this essence is important take fringed Violet. Very useful in cases of schizophrenia, hallucinations and all forms of psychosis as it deadens the negative entity of self-destructive messages.

The essence is also capable of relieving those umbilical cords "energetic" that yes they establish at the birth between people with constraints affective close. When a person give there own power without reserves could feel empty, tired And in this case Angelsword can   to be Jack orally as well as applied topically between the navel and the sternum.

Autumn leaves

Autumn Leaves is prepared exclusively from leaves harvested in Autumn in the moment exact in which they abandon theirs tree.
The essence is mainly used for people who are staying leaving this world, as it eases the transition from the plane physical to the spiritual world. In the last days of life, a person is helped to become aware of his own condition And to remember the loved ones in the world spiritual.

- The essence allows you to listen and feel the contact with the afterlife and Of to be open during the ride with there awareness of help Of a guide And presence of much love around.

Banksia Robur

It belongs at the family of the Proteaceae, fifty different especially throughout Australia. The denomination "robur" derives from Latin and means strong. The flowers are greenish blue in colour in the beginning and then turn yellow when the plant opens e remains cover Of flowers. It grows in marshy areas of ribs.

- It is the remedy for temporary tiredness, with a mild feeling of frustration or defeat.

Normally, these people I am dynamics, with great power and enthusiasm, but for different reasons (disease, exhaustion, disappointment), yes they feel temporarily cut down or discouraged.

- Useful in the syndrome from tiredness chronic.

Since this is one state little frequent in this type Ofpeople, the they live like something Of strange and maddening And they wish get out of it the more soon possible. The flower is very usefulto overcome the frustration associated with the decrease in energy of this period.

- To do bathrooms in which he comes addition the essence increase the action of the remedy.

The flower gives a renewed interest in life and in the joy of to live. Reports joy And interest in the life after, or even during, a disease. How this shrub that prefers the swampy moorlands of southern Australia, the essence isable to do get the person out of the swamp in which he is momentarily to return on a ground solid.

Bauhinia

Tree that can come as far as 10 meters Of height, Of trunk short, massive, covered with colored fissured bark dark gray. The hanging branches give an idea of transience. Leaves I am wide, ovals, Of color greenish-blue to form Of butterfly. From June to September the tree lose the leaves, but appear the flowers little ones, velvety And Of color orange-red. The personality Bauhinia has how characteristic there rigidity of the character. This translates into resistance to changes, to new ones ideas, to accept ways and habits different from their own. This psychic constellation arises from a need to defend, deny or repress emotions that the individual experiences as dangerous, of way such that the character rigid And hardened can to be a consequence and a form to ensure the maintenance of barriers against excluded emotions. This rigidity is expressed in two main areas: new ideas and different people. They are people who tend to reject or feel a sense of alienation from everything what is new or different. Inability to accept changes closed-mindedness, rigidity and bigotry. Even for those who struggle to to adapt at new technologies modern. The flower it helps the people to become more flexible in the view and conception of things and more open to considering new points of view. Loss of prejudices and open-mindedness towards new concepts, situations e ideas.
For eliminate the Images restrictive And self imposed that a individual has built on self same because is convinced Of not be the type of person who can perform certain activities such as dance or paint.
TO level physicist there Bauhinia restore there functionality of the ileocecal valve which is the valve that separates the pyrole from the large intestine, the point where they usually undermine bacteria. The PH of the small intestine is basic, while the large is acid so the imbalance from the valve is responsible from the most intestinal disorders such as bloating, bloating, fermentation, intolerances food.

Billy Goat Plum

In woodland it grows in width, like a shrub small size, while in humid places, it becomes a large one tree, up to 10 meters tall, with thick, gnarled bark and grey. The leaves are oval, light green in color and, towards the end from the season dry, first Of to fall they become Of a red brilliant. THE flowers scented I am big And fleshy, with long lobescalyx green and white or yellow petals. The numerous, long stamens yes they develop from a reddish base and, towards the tips, become whites. The flowering period begins in July and ends at October. The Aboriginal people used the inner bark of the tree (pounded and soaked in water until it turned red), for disinfect pustules, burns And sores. The thin And smallroots were soaked in water and applied to the skin for relieve the itch in case Of prickly heat of the children And of chickenpox.

- The essence is specific to feelings of aversion or repulsion towards self themselves, especially when I am aimed at the organs or the sexual act it carries with it feelings Of guilt And Sin.

There I am emotions Of loathing, aversion, disapproval of oneself, fear associated to the past, shame for there own sexuality, senses Of guilt, need Of punishment, feelings of impurity, anger And hate repressed.
With respect to sexuality, the essence is useful in cases where the person manifests inability to enjoy, feels dirty or repugnant towards sex. Coldness is associated with fear and denial of pleasure. Self these emotions they interfere negatively with the deed sexual, can override the feeling that the body is dirty and unattractive to the partner; the essence helps to make a real acceptance of physicality, allowing you to enjoy the sensations physical And of the pleasures sexual. In the case in which a rash cutaneous or an elimination Of toxins through there skin (sweat, cycle menstruation, vaginal flow) is experienced with disgust and/or embarrassment.
Indicated for Everything is fine sensation Of aversion

towards self themselves or your own physique.

- The essence helps to gain awareness that in people there is something more, beyond appearance, and that looking deeply it is possible to see the authentic beauty.

It can be taken orally or applied topically, for pathologies skin Which the eczema or there psoriasis, provided these involve the feeling that the body is not enough clean. Useful used locally in epidermal affections, such as acne. Very useful in the periods of adolescence in which the problematic Of not acceptance of the own body I am amplified: acne, pimples, body loathing and non-acceptance of sexual development. In eating disorders to heal any kind of shame, self-loathing or loathing of themselves and of the body.
Difficulty communicating with someone you are attracted to why you feel embarrassed or complexed; the feeling of shame for a own particular appearance holds from interacting or to communicate with the other.

Black Eyes Susan

For who has a temper hyperactive and characterized from a constant mental work. They are people who are impatient with the pace too slow than the others. It is useful when you feel that the time is never enough and the pace of life is always stressful. The flower allows you to reorganize your own life rhythms and to find the weather for self themselves. Raise awareness towards the other, demonstrating kindness, sympathy, patience and listening skills. For who is it always in movement, not yes rests or he is sleeping enough, generally pushes beyond their physical and emotional limits. For people who are unrealistic about the weather; I am convinced that in future they will have enough weather for to read or for Do all the things who are hoarding.

For people who live in the city and are always running, active and energetic and no yes stop never.

When there is a need to detach from the frenzy of a world external And find a little' Of silence inner.

For impulsivity: impatience to get things done can lead to hasty decisions, without evaluating the consequences to long term.

For problems Of insomnia due to hyper dynamism.

- THE symptoms physical for which use the essence I am in relation to the apparatus digestive, intestinal with frequent episodes Of dysentery, headaches, muscle tension, back pain, pathologies from attention deficit, insomnia, hyper kinesia even in children.

The essence sensitizes towards the other giving kindness, patience, ability of listening And tolerance.

Bluebells

It belongs at the family of the Campanulaceae that it means "little bell" in Latin. It is a perennial herb half a meter high, with a few small and soft leaves and blue-violet flowers. She is a native of the Olgas Katajuta, as the aborigines recall geographical center of Australia. For fear of contacting the sphere of feelings for fear of dispersing them. Thus emotions result unexpressed and one no longer has the hope of being able to live them as in precedence. This creates a sort of isolation from people dear. I'm people that not by hand to exhibit there own personality because they think that this could not to be cheap. AND' useful for the children that not they want to share their own toys with the other.

- The flower opens the heart, laugh there joy And there wants Of emotional participation with others. The Bluebell people they possess a closed to free personality structure expression of emotions and feelings.

The reason for this repression is the unconscious fear that their affective world vibrates in a way that is not reciprocated or including. Another major fear is the possibility of getting to a state of material shortage. This leads them to develop a greedy and possessive behavior. The way by which these personalities try to control "the letting go", "the give" is by installing hard, controlled, coating character traits of brutal frankly their language.
The flower opens the heart so that emerge emotions contained and we may learn that true abundance consists in giving. Bluebell is indicated to all who they have blocked the doors of the heart because it helps to remove the barriers environment to the chakras of the heart.

- Very useful in the departments Of cardiology or for everyone those that they suffer interventions surgical Of bypass, transplant Of heart, hypertension, in how much remove blocks environment to the chakras.

Boab

Yup deals with of the baobab Australian that grows in Australia western in plains sandy where is it there I am abundant rainfall, or long the ridges rocky, the lines Of drainage and streams. During the dry season, it loses its leaves, but first of arrival of the rains yes covers Of long leaves alternate and compound whose upper page is green, while that whitish underside and have up to 9 pointed lobes, hairy and tapered. It flowers from November to February. The flowers are large up to 12 cm in height and width, composed of 5 fleshy petals of color White cream And they have numerous, long stamens.

- In legends Of many cultures, there form of the baobab iscompared to that of an overturned tree, whose crown is develop in the ground And the roots grow in the air.

One legend compares it to a whale with its head sunk in the land and the whale is associated with family, as much as it is the Boab tree. In Australian Aboriginal tribes, if a childbirth occurred during flowering, the tribe collected the flowers and there gave to the woman who walked away, dug a hole and covered them his walls of the flowers, so yes squatted on the hole And gave birth the baby in a baby cot flowery. The first contact of the child was with these flowers that break negative patterns handed down by generation in generation.

- There property Of this flower is that Of eliminate the negative thought patterns resulting from one's heritage familiar, or all those manifestations And beliefs that are rooted and transmitted from generation to generationin generation.

It is a useful essence to find what you are, eliminating layers of models And thoughts obsolete. For who broods on experiences negative of the past. It helps the parents to to be more tolerant with their own children, because it blocks the projection of all their desires and the expectations not accomplished.

Boronia

The Boronias belong to the Rutaceae family (the same family that comprehends lemons, oranges, limes).
For who has thoughts obsessive recurring from which not succeeds to to break free. This remedy it helps to quiet down there mind, allowing to to increase their own abilities intuitive.
Useful when yes addresses attention in way obsessive towards another person, for example after breaking up with the partner.

- The people Boronia yes they feel dominate from ideas obsessive And thoughts fixed give her Which not can break away.

The reason for this fixation is due to various reasons, but between they must underline there frustration, the difficulty in accepting loss and suffering. I'm people generally sad, And "ruminants mental."
An expression of this picture is insomnia of which normally suffer, the disconnection in daily tasks and the loss of creativity. Another trait to take into account is the difficulty in the be able to associate or report thoughts freely.
This is due to the fact that the Boronia put themselves "on guard" from avoiding sure thoughts or central ideas that they don't want either see neither to listen. Paradoxically, this would be an exit of his continuous mental rumination. The emotions present in the state Boronia I am: there fear Of to choose there own direction in life, stifled hate, a block in the past, denial a giving up old ideas, lack of spontaneity, desire to control for insecurity, possession, depression, sadness, suffering, self-compassion And mental torture.
It is very specific for those people who feel stuck in ideas how a disk Broken that continues to spin in the They headso that they permanently remember situations or conversations. This there brings to deconcentration.

Bottle Brush

These are people who are walking paths of change And transformations, but for this yes they generally feel with little hope in one's own ability to cope effectively new situations.
Useful in all moments of transition such as the marriage, pregnancy, birth, menopause, death itself.
The flower helps sweep away the past, inviting the person to receive new experiences And new situations.
To allow you to experience life and its inevitable changes, making capable Of exceed constructively the past And walking happily towards new ones experiences.
The essence promotes the bond between mother and child and helps in the menopause, when yes has fear Of not to be desired And Of grow old.

- This essence is very useful in old age to accept the change that it involves for the individual physical, psychic and social transformations to which yes see forced.

IS the remedy from not administer to the children in how much the experiences until to the 12 years are based on naturalness.
Bottlebrush invites people to experience life and its inevitables changes allowing Of exceed the past in way constructive towards the future.

- TO level physicist acts in way optimal on colon And everyone the disturbances to it connected how there syndrome from colon irritable purifying it And draining it give her slag.

Bush Fuchsia

Remedy important in problems Of learning.
Allows the integration Of both of them the hemispheres cerebral, solving there majority Of problems Of learning that come from imbalances between the two hemispheres (dyslexia, stuttering, difficulty to articulate the oral language, aphasia).
It helps in having safety in the speak in public.
Inability Of to balance the side logical And rational with that intuitive And creative. Inability to feel or follow the instinct.
Useful in cases of inability to study for long periods without lose focus. By balancing the two cerebral hemispheres, it helps to enter in contact with their own insights.
It helps to find there capacity Of distinguish And Of to interpret theinformation and the perceptions.

- It helps to develop intuition and to have self-confidence instinct.

For who is very weather front to video terminals or other devices electronic And yes hear a bit' clouded to end day.
This flower enhances speech and communicative clarity as well donate the necessary security to talk in public.
Increase the capacity Of concentration And so Ofunderstanding of a text or material Of study.
Increase the wish Of to read in the children And increases also your own trust and safety in class and of in front of exams.
How stimulates the development of the functions logics And rational (left cerebral hemisphere), it will also do so with the creative aspects And intuitive, matching to the hemisphere right brain.
Allows Of to balance the function Of both of them the hemispheres when there is an excessive dominance Of one on the other.
Another aspect of this essence is its ability to facilitate the coordination of movements. Another property, the relation with the expression verbal, is that it helps in the conversation improving the tone, the inflection And the melody of the voice.

It also improves hearing ability, especially in cases of infections chronic. Useful in the rebalancing of the hypothalamus, subsequently to you use prolonged Of pills contraceptives or treatment substitute hormonal.

Excellent for tuning into one's intuition, for the coordination hand-eye And for there capacity Of express ideas, allows people to believe in own intuition and in one's own way of acting, rather what to do that that they say the other.

- In the case of dyslexia, it is necessary to take Bush Fuchsia for 15 consecutive days and repeat the treatment after an interruption of a pair Of weeks. IS the essence of choice of the pituitary.

Great for infections earphones, dizziness, mazes and nausea.

Bush Gardenia

Although it is possible to describe a flower type Bush Gardenia, more that a framework Of personality yes deals with Of a state emotional that is characterized by difficulty and deterioration in relations affective And in the problems Of communication interpersonal. It unites the people that yes they stand driving away emotionally, mostly for incommunicability.
They are generally selfish and busy with their activities, they have little interest and are overly demanding of others. They live focused on their concerns, goals and objectives, without being able to detach oneself from them, without being able to look at who is there surrounds, And so the people that there surround yes they feel forget. They have to learn to invest the They weather for understand the other.

- Helps to bring estranged couples closer together because too worry from the respective existences.

It is as if the essence leads individuals to look at each other, a see what your partner is doing and feeling, as well as a figure out what it serves for get closer.
IS also remarkable the action ameliorative Of this flower in the interest And in the wish sexual when there monotony And the obvious yes. I am insinuated in a report.
This remedy is not only indicated for love relationships man-woman, but also for the family ties.
It can be used when a family member upsets the own existence due to drugs or other problems, while the the rest of the family remains unaware of it, because they are too absorbed give your own engagements personal.

Bush Iris

Fear from the death, materialism, rejection from the spirituality, denial Of everything that is that it is material, atheism, extremism.
Perception spiritual of the individual And from the reality to the Of there of thematerial plan And physicist.

- Allows to the individual Of log into at the own spiritual dimension and to open the doors of their own perceptions more ends. Allows that there faith you penetrate in the deep of the individual.

These are people who suffer from a deep attachment to possessions materials. misers, worldly, generally they have a conception atheist from the life. Can have also traits Of intellectualism, disbelief and excessive realism.
The main emotions that they live I am: avarice, fear, insecurity, possessiveness, frustration, dissatisfaction, block, little sensitivity And scarce capacity Of get excited.
The main function of this flower is the development of life spiritual, the amplification from the consciousness And the fight there fear to death. Increase there perception.
When the individual has to develop his spiritual life why find pleasure alone in excesses And in the satisfaction of the own need, how can to be addictions, sex, supply. IS a optimal remedy in the cases in patients terminals or dominated for there fear at the death relieving the anguish And there suffering connected to this transition.

Christmas Bell

Sense Of lost be emotional that material.
To help manifest one's desires, for those who have a sense Of
lack be to level emotional that material.
- The very name of the flower "Christmas bells"
  corresponds to a time of year that is traditionally
  associated with at the joy in the give And in the to
  receive, love And gifts, that they symbolize peace in
  ties affective.

Crowea

This flower has a powerful calming effect on the mind and body body, for anxiety and stress, giving an intense feeling of Welfare And quiet. Concerns, lost of balance, lack Of safety Of self themselves, sensation Of not to be enough adequate. Anxiety. The flower give there rediscovered of individual equilibrium and a renewed contact with one's own feelings. This personality is characterized from to be habitually dissatisfied with herself, deconcentrated, discontented. They live with obsessive worrying and are gripped by a vague feeling of fear and panic that is neither defined nor concrete. I'm people who find it difficult to be happy or to relax, therefore they are often Of bad humor And cranky.

- There lesson that sign this flower is that Of not to live worry incessantly.

It is an excellent flower for personalities hypochondriacs and excessively worry for everything. I'm people who do not know how to assimilate reality and events and that does in way that does not they can't either to assimilate well the foods.
They also often suffer from insomnia and cannot relax all the time because they are unable to enjoy life and release tension. This voltage constant the power of attorney a ache indoor very deep that not accept to level self conscious And wants hold hidden and also embodies a feeling of inferiority, and of guilt.
Great for there syndrome premenstrual.
Crowea is also excellent for ulcer and other ailments of the stomach as a regulator of gastric acidity. Has also effect on muscles, tendons. Useful in cases of asthma, bronchial spasms and pain in the intercostal muscles. Crowea it turns out to be a excellent instrument for theeternally anxious.

Daggers Hakea

These are individuals dominated by intense feelings of bitterness and resentment towards people who are very close to or with States tied up emotionally, family members, comrade, friends.
They are people who are a bit pungent and who sometimes use words sharp or for those who still feel old hidden grievances which they keep within themselves, while in parallel they develop a mask of appearance tender And sweet.
Inability Of forgive And Of forget.
Sense of bitterness towards a closed family, the friends and of their own Dear.
Rediscovered from the capacity Of forgive And Of to express openly i own feelings.

- Favors processing And there result resolution Of particular situations full of resentment and hatred in which they are involved relationships interpersonal important.

This flower is very useful in relationships that ended badly or in quarrels family members, especially self the individual is dominated from feelings Of resentment, bitterness And sensation Of to be state treated unfairly.

- TO level physicist detox the liver draining it.

Dog Rose

For who has fear or suffers Of phobias. For the shy And the apprehensive.For who is it nagged from fears unfounded.
The flower laugh trust And safety in self themselves.
It helps to discover a renewed courage to face others and the ability to embrace and enjoy fully the life.
- The Dog Rose personality has being as its central characteristic dominated by a deep feeling of fear for the things of the life daily.

These fear reflects a lack Of self esteem and courage. Other significant traits are the shyness that can translate in stutter, there conduct inhibited that normally manifests insecurity, anxiety, and apprehension about others. He lives there feeling that there is no direction in which to advance that he discovers an emotional nucleus linked to distrust of life and fear of future and this brings anger and anguish with himself for his own insecurities, beyond that apprehension.
Dog Rose gives these people more confidence with the own world inner And Consequently allows a greater freedom of expression.
- The consequences of the fears to level psychic I am consist for many of stomach problems that can degenerate in ulcers from hyperacidity.

Constant fears can also weaken the functionality of adrenal glands and decrease the amount of oxygen in the body. Dog Rose is useful in case of insomnia or nightmares. Very useful for the hypochondria.

Dog Rose of Wilde Force

They are people who are very afraid of losing control, yes they feel invaded from emotions intense.
They think they can commit madness and many times this is there brings to be excessively rigid And control yourself.
When there yes find to to live a situation pervasive or emotionally charge accompanied, for example from a contagious hysteria collective.
Suffering without a cause apparent.

- There function Of this essence is to increase self-control And there capacity Of take contact with the unconscious.

The flower give calm, equilibrium emotional, capacity Of check the intensity of the riots interior or the manifestations exterior of the themselves

Five Corners

Essence addressed at lessons universal of self-esteem And of acceptance Of self for win back there confidence with there own beauty inner and exterior.
It is the remedy of celebration of physical being and essence of the individual And it helps to feel sure from the own beauty inner and exterior.
People who don't feel comfortable with themselves they have the feeling of being crushed by world and harm often the impression to do Of everything to not get noticed.

- Above all, the flower favors self-acceptance and, of consequence, the acceptance from the beauty of the own to be to everyone the levels.

I'm people that they suffer deeply Of a terrible fear of life and acceptance of that which they are.
How consequence, there They life Of relationship not is happy.
It lacks They cheerfulness And heat, And yes they entail in a way content. The devaluation of his own body is a reflex of the insecurity that there dominates.

- There function Of this essence is give trust, cure there devaluation and make the person feel in harmony with their own body. To increase the to flow of energy vital.

Flannel Flower

It grows in rocky and sandy areas. The whole plant is covered with a soft and silky fluff reminiscent of flannel. Foliage branched, velvety, opposite deeply lobed. The flower that very reminiscent of the Edelweiss, with white velvety petals and with the green tip, appears from spring to late summer.
For those who do not like physical contact with others and are not at own comfortable with there own physical intimacy and emotional.
For who find difficulty to express to words the own feelings.

- The flower it helps there discovery from the capacity Of to enjoy Of all the manifestations physical and especially sensitivity to the contact physicist with the other And resizing of the own borders.

Renew trust in expressing And reveal self themselves garlic other, through there sensuality And sweetness.
This essence defines a characteristic guy psychological floral where the person manifests a difficulty in putting himself in body contact. This leads him to escape physical contact it's at to be miserly in the give And to receive caresses.
They are people who normally appear different than they they are actually, in fact seem to have a possibility of grand gestures of affection. Instead this is not real and if the caresses are present I am forced or is little deep the lived indoor that there accompanies. It's all about seduction which is normally a stretch Of personality narcissistic And not a real interest for the other.
IS common find also a block that hinders there free expression of affection. The main function of this essence is give there capacity to enjoy of the body contact, Of to be free in expression of the feelings, tender And to hear positively the skin contact to skin.

Fresh Water Mangrove

For people that they have prejudices not based on experience personal, but handed down of generation in generation.
It is the remedy indicated for those who have already prepared certain schemes of thinking about something or someone (e.g. the forms of racial or religious intolerance). The flower gives humility and openness towards new experiences, people And feelings.
- It helps to discover the Nice that characterizes Everything is fine person And to get rid of prejudices.

A wise individual is one who can perceive and accept new knowledge and theories or see a new reality considering the things from a new prospect.
- This flower is useful in the acceptance of others when there's a prejudice mental preformed.

Opens the heart when there is a bias to hearsay, but not for experience direct, when the expectation Of how the what's this I amor they should to be block the perception of reality.
For the individual who has been taught by his family to hate girls people Of a particular race or religion, but that not has none experience personal for share them.

Fringed Violet

The state fringed Violet yes characterizes from existence Of a traumatic experience or a shock that has damaged the framework psychic and energy of the individual.
Situations in which yes is suffered for a attack external that has procured one tore up indoor And this does to emerge there vulnerability in facing that attack that brought a great pain and depression related to the unprocessed trauma and of which they haven't recovered yet. Flooded by this experience of pain, the individual lives with a fear growing at the reiteration of the negative experience. For a period after birth, the aura of the newborn is open, like the anterior fontanelle.
For protect her give it influences negative, yes can to apply a few drops Of fringed Violet in that point.
This essence is very useful to those that they have right away amputation and may develop some ailment from the awareness bodily, how there syndrome from limbghost.
fringed Violet keeps integrates there protection of the individual, blocking in this way the energies unwanted externals.

- It's great for people who let themselves be drained by other, as well as for those that unconsciously they absorbthe imbalances physical and emotions of others.

Exhaustion provoke yourself from people and events (how radiation)that there surround. The flower removes the effects of the concerns of the here I'm and of the past. It protects there psyche.

- Fringed Violet is used in conjunction with Flannel Flower for abuse suffered by men and together with Wisteria for the abuses on women.

Green Essence

He comes prepared with stems And leaves Of traditional herbs greens fresh according to the same method used for preparation of the flower essences (solar method).
- Useful essence to clean up and purify the body by helping it eliminate the excessive fermentation, molds and parasites.

Topically can   favor the elimination of problems skin like eczema And fungal infections.
Place 7 drops of Green Essence in a small bowl with a little water and wet the affected area leaving to dry. Repeat this operation twice a day for two weeks. After this cycle, yes can, possibly to continue the application Of this treatment external, Everything is fine two days.
- As an oral intake, it is recommended to use for two weeks, 7 drops, five minutes before meals (3 times a day) for a period Of 2 weeks.

Not match use topical And oral of the essence.

Green Spiders Orchid

Nightmares And phobias due to experiences of the past.Reaction exaggerated at the sight of blood.
Inability Of to come in in communication not alone with the people,but also with other living being And other size spiritual.

- The flower favors the expression Of potential capacity extrasensory. It allows you to connect with all beings living And with people Of languages different.

Grey Spiders Flower

AND' the flower for the States Of terror, panic, nightmares, Associates to extreme and destabilizing anxiety. It is a type of fear that brings pupils dilate, throat dry, tachycardia, a fear immobilizing. Useful in children's nightmares in which the fear persists for hours also after the awakening.

- Indicated in panic attacks, donate trust, courage And calm.

Useful in cases Of terror from claustrophobia or agoraphobia, when yes they have phobias And yes has fear Of remain terrified, for have courage in situations scary, in the pregnancy for the terror of the childbirth, for the terror result to shock or trauma.

TO part the terror extreme, the panic, there despair And there fear at the what supernatural there is also one state Of alert permanent, the expectation of imminent danger and the lack of trust And Of faith in self themselves. These reactions yes they produce faced with extreme situations, such as the threat of death, war or Of forehead to that is that is unknown. In these circumstances, there person hear that there her life And there her identity yes they find in danger.

- It is important to keep in mind which fear over which work this essence is the one that arrives suddenly and yes it takes possession of the individual, disorganizing and paralyzing him.

However, it also acts as a preventative, for example, in those people who have to carry out a risky job that needs of the development Of a great courage for face up to situations potentially but really dangerous.

Gymea Lily

The essence is useful for drawing from our energy and obtaining the force Of to be themselves and of Do that is that needs to to be done.

- It is an aid to fully realize one's destiny superior, discover there passion from the own life And follow her, doing that that does vibrate the heart.

Ian White says: "It's the remedy for those who wish to lead a life extraordinary, flying tall how the eagles, without get trapped - like chickens in coops - in the torpor of mediocrity and in the oblivion of reality of consent".
Because the chickens, At bottom, they know that staying too much to long in the coop they lose the ability to fly and begin to envy the eagles soaring overhead. Our beliefs, which are comfortable for us and which form the basis and structure of the our society are limiting and generated by fear. They come transmitted since childhood and continuously reinforced by the masses media and there is no encouragement to create the reality within from the own life. Self we have a point Of view And abelief different from those of the other or we have very success in life, the essence helps to maintain determination and the focus on doing what you know you should do, with a such decisiveness that not yes is for nothing worry of opinion or of judgment of the others on the self.
A appearance from the doctrine of the signatures of the flower is that is so tall that it is not clearly distinguishable from the ground beyond that unreachable for those who are to the its feet.

- It is therefore also suitable for individuals with a strong personality outgoing or for those who are dominant, charismatic and used to it to go for there own Street.

Generally these individuals are natural leaders, not have difficulty taking control of a situation ea make decisions on the fly without even thinking about it and want to take control to make things work better (not for authoritarianism). Gymea Lily attenuates this trend, inducing the subjects to to evaluate self is appropriate, or actually necessary, take on a task. It also helps them to be more aware of the other, avoiding Of trample them, And to recognizethat people actually want to contribute in their own way, too if a times not is same to you dynamic or efficient.

- Gymea Lily is indicated also for the behaviors targeted to get attention and for the constant desire to charm. Can to help to to commute in humility the excessive pride And the arrogance.

Another one peculiarity Of this essence is Of to break down the barriers of fear and trepidation that an individual can have against people in power, favoring a rapprochement and sharing of ideas between two counterparts.

- The essence in this case has a Double action very interesting: it transforms the negative thoughts you have towards people oppressors in positive, and dissolves there fear that inspire.

Thought is very powerful, oppressors create situations of captivity, but exists a responsibility also in who suffers oppression, as it is due to the perpetuation of patterns of thought negatives that indirectly there yes poses in a position Of passivity. dissolving these negativity, the essence create there opportunity for the oppressed to really change, thus freeing themselves from the her itself captivity.

Hibbertia

For those who devour information and philosophies and who have a great wish Of learn, studying constantly books And participating in courses. These are extremely strict subjects with self themselves, especially in the They continuous Chase of learning that often It tends to make them fanatics.
However, all the information does not derive from direct experience and this carries the risk of not having a real understanding and knowledge from the matter.
I'm personality rigid and excessively self-disciplined, get excited give your own successes.

- The essence give the acceptance of the own limits And there rediscoveredthe need to deepen and enrich one's knowledge and philosophies Of life.

Illawara Flame Tree

It is indicated for those people who feel rejected, left in aloof, do not love. For those who ignore their potential and have fear of responsibility. They are people who know what they have to do, but feel burdened with the responsibility of doing so. The flower give self-acceptance, trust in self themselves and force inner.

When the rejection, fictional or real, he comes manifested, there person is deeply hurt, with a feeling of abandonment. For to avoid possible waste they do what's this that not they would like to do. They know they possess certain skills, but they're not into it degree of develop them or exploit them.

They ignore the own potential, making himself exempt from the responsibility Of apply them to themselves.

- The essence it helps to Do the promo step towards there realization of the own potential, does take confidence with the true aspirations from the life without feel crushed by responsibility.

I'm people that they tend also to to decline self themselves falling, sometimes, in a state Of depression.

Great for children because it can help in situations of exclusion, such as from the soccer team or the dominant group or that they come entered in a new school where is it, self teachers and comrades do not pay much attention to him, they live this situation how a rejection And instead Of search for Of Do friendship, they get discouraged. These subjects are characterized by a particular characteristic psychological in whichself-marginalization, suffering in the face of rejection and fear from the responsibility form there central structure of the painting.

Another characteristic trait is the intense apprehension of new things situations or experiences. Without a doubt, these personalities are very insecure And constantly needy Of to be love And accept. They suffer very Of to be leave outside from a situation, that be generated from something Of extreme or simply treat yourself simply Of a done irrelevant from the life at the which none other person would give importance.

Much there conduct apprehensive that there fear to exclusion there they bring to develop a behavior offender with there people, although in reality this attitude be a defence front to the ache deep that they have caused the disappointments affective, the abuse lack to be taken in consideration.

- The main function of this essence is to give confidence, capacity Of compromise, force internal, car approval.

It helps to face the first step in new situations e takes away there fear of exclusion And of the rejection.

- This flower work very well in situations in which there are difficulties and fears in taking responsibility new, like the paternity, the marriage.

Also useful in menopause where one can feel devalued, with there sensation Of not to be desirable And for this to be rejected.

Isopogon

This flower it helps to recover the memory of the past.
For the people that they wish remember skills or informationlearned years ago. For who is unable Of learn give her experiences of the past. Useful also for the people stubborn And authoritarians who do not trust others, for very strict parents. Individuals that they have need Of dominate And check the other with a constant supervision And not they succeed neither toto imagine that someone other may carry out a worksame to you well, or really better than They.
They often feel they know more than others. They are dominated people from the They intellect And that present a clear separation betweenheart and mind.

- The flower makes it possible to learn from lived experiences, to remember the past and of recover the skills lost

Inability Of learn from experience. Bad memory. Yup characterized by having a stubborn and manipulative personality. They are people who are very centered in their intellectual life and completely separated from theirs world affective.
Usually dominant, there They closure mental And there dissociation there leads to learn little or nothing of the experiences, so that they live repeating errors.
These people yes they feel strongly tied to the They criteria And beliefs hardened And with little elasticity Of thought And this it doesn't make them accept the changes e difficult to adapt to what new. Generally I am people rigid, criticisms, bitter And with an intense repression of the They worldemotional.

Jacaranda

Constantly undecided people find it hard to be able to choose easily, they doubt always and change their mind.
Normally they begin many what's this And not neither they finish none. In some cases there is also a marked feeling of indifference to life. The structure of these people is spinning environment to lack of confidence in that is that they think And I am.
Sometimes they consult other people looking for answers to their doubts and uncertainties, but hardly the answers that they receive there they motivate to stop Of to doubt.
Other traits of the character I am the permanent nervousness, there dispersion, the wavering tone with which they express themselves and the lack of goals in their life, sometimes accompanied by a strong state of confusion And disorientation.
The main function of this essence is to give abilities of decision. Also clarity and mental quickness.

- It is the remedy for people starting their projects and they do not complete them, mainly because they are distracted from others sources Of information.

Suitable for those who have great difficulty making decisions, because it changes constantly idea.
For those who want to be a bit everywhere, without following a specific oneand alone direction.
I'm people very insecure on which be there right Street from take, other times they panic thinking they have made the choice wrong. The flower give decision, lucidity mental, concentration And lucidity Of thought.

Kangaroos Paw

It is used for people whose extreme naivety leads to clumsiness and difficulty relating to others caused by feeling of to be limited or outside place.
Useful also for the people insensitive that pose excessive questions to others or that does not they look problems others.

- This flower sensitizes towards the needs of the other people, gives the ability to feel good about people with different pasts and personalities and allows you to understand that that others need by making them feel relaxed e take comfort.

For who not knows the rules behavioral of the to live in company, appearing clumsy And embarrassed And insensitive.
The flower relax, from sensitivity And "savoir faire", it helps in the rediscovery of the pleasure of being with others. It is a valid essence even for those who always know what is right to say, but not they manage to express it out of insecurity or lack of courage.

- And the remedy that helps to understand how to act appropriately in all situations.

They are personalities with difficulty integrating social and inexperienced in relating to people. The interaction is a serious problem for them. Too self-centered at times selfish, not they perceive with ease the need And the requests of those that surround them.
This leads them to appear as numb, which is more owed to the lack of conscience or the clumsiness that in the presence of negative emotions. Another characteristic feature is the lack of ability to listen. With little "savoir faire", normally not they are seen by others as attractive individuals to make contacts and communication.
They are reluctant to socialize that they avoid the relations. The from nuisance there presence Of a group. Little flexible in the They manner Of think, I am stubborn And not they accept easily

a difference of opinions.
Very inconsiderate And scratchy in their conversations, they try Of to avoid Of to stay in groups And the relations I am generally superficial. Inexperienced, crude, stubborn, afraid to be ridiculous like this they hold distant the people.
Underlying these personalities is 'insecurity, devaluation and disqualification Of themselves.
The functions more important Of this flower I am give to the individual a greater ability to perceive the signs that others emit, increase its sensitivity and have good level Of "feeling" in relations interpersonal.

Kapok Bush

For those who are easily discouraged. When effort is required, yes they do inevitable there demoralization And the felling. Resignation And apathy.
- The flower gives perseverance and I commit. Determine goodwill for react to state Of apathy.

The greatest unease appears, indeed, there lack Of force Of will, because everything seems too tiring and these people they emanate sadness, depression and end up surrounding themselves with a monotonous and depressing atmosphere. This remedy helps to respond positively to life changes, invites you not to give up, ad keep going until the solution is found.
For commitment, perseverance, never give up and never accept defeat, the destiny.
For children, who in the school environment, do not even try to face up to a subject because there they find too difficult.
- Kapok Bush helps to react positively to the challenges oflife.

- For those that they possess a low resistance at the frustration they are easily discouraged and declare themselves vanquished in front of the majority small obstacle that appears to him. Their typical reactions are those of resignation, discouragement and apathy. Behind this mask hides the fear of living, the feeling of not worth enough. Defeatism is another significant trait ofcharacter of the Kapok Bushes.

The feeling of "for what reason? what's the point of doing all this, I'm useless"? joins a intense feeling Of to be oppressed come on loads from the life. Normally yes they find, in the history Of these people, strong deficiencies affective And Of love in childhood.

The emotions own Of this flower I am: discouragement, apathy, resignation, discouragement, discouragement, depression, sensation Of feel won, fear at the life, devaluation, resistance to change things, fear of death, resentment preserved, gnawed from affliction, overwhelmed, sense Of guilt.

Lichen

It helps to be aware to seek hope and Light in the moment from the death physics.
It assists in the separation that takes place between the physical body and the body etheric at the moment of death and pressed to free himself from energies that hold ties with the terrestrial world and create a sense Of disorientation Of forehead to the border between the world terrestrial and the plan spiritual.

Little Flannel Flower

For who refuses the child that is inside Of self.
It allows you to express playfulness and freedom of thought. It helpsrecover the innocence And there desire of to play.
Excellent remedy for parents as it helps them to surrender toself same demonstrating Of know still   what does it want to say to play Andfor children who have grown up too fast and tend to Do own the sorry about the world.
Useful also for those children that they look a lot television and listen to news and negative events that they give one vision sad, painful And negative.

- The flower gives the rediscovery of innocence, of the desire to to play And Of joke, to have fun and Of to be spontaneous

They are personalities who normally perceive life and things with too shady and serious a perspective. The concern there dominates And not can leave to emerge there spontaneity And the baby inner. Many times they seem deprived Of vitality And unable to enjoy games he was born in playful sense of life.
With little sense of humor, they intellectualize the They emotions and it's as if they carry a great weight in the his heart.
They appear to be several years older than their royals. The look denotes pain, suffering, distress and lack of pleasure.
I'm people rigid And self-criticism, it costs They see the side good of things. They pay attention to disasters and accidents Of every kind. It costs them, though they are attentive to suffering, to giveaffection or do something that has to do with doing good tosuffering. THE children I am scholars, they play little, not I am interested in sports, prefer research, chess, to go in square or to play with a pet. Adults experience the world with excessive demands, corrections, severity, routine and a sense of duty. Both children and adults are boring. The flower's lesson is to learn to to be spontaneous And leave that the our baby indoor yes express without fear.

Macrocarpa

AND' a remedy for the energy, there vitality And there resistence physics.

For exhausted, tired and depressed people. Renew the enthusiasm, vitality and energy. Excellent tonic for those who need to "pull themselves su", can be taken at a time of great physical stress, when is necessary there resistance or how much yes is reached a difficult destination and you are so exhausted that you cannot enjoy the success.

Great for the people in convalescence.

But it is important not to lose sight of the fact that this exhaustion is not only physical, but also mental, because not only there person not can Do, but not even manages to think.

- The Macrocarpa is characterized by the lack of resistance, the lack Of force And vitality And there vulnerability much in the They system immune as in the psychic defensive ones that leave them with a low level Of self-protection.

Normally they accumulate inside They a loud power negative emotion, defeatism and a tendency to neglect there treatment from the own person, how self they had given up unconsciously a to continue.

They have great difficulty limiting themselves, but they try hard and they exceed beyond the their chance.

They believe to 60 years Of have there itself power of the 20; not they know or not they want to be aware of the They limits And they arrive in stressful situations without understanding the stimuli they are in the They indoor.

Mint Bush

Disorder, confusion, disorientation and "inner alarm". Start Of a turmoil and of a void spiritual.
resize, smooth out, harmonize.
It helps to find clarity, calm And skills in the manage the situations also spiritual.

- Mint Bush is optimal when there yes find in a period Of perturbations as if wandering constantly on one side to another in confusion and in the dilemma, such as when Yes is undecided whether to continue a relationship or interrupt her.

Mint Bush it helps to manage with efficiency situations particularly loaded Of voltage.
It is for a period during which it happens to harness energies beyond the own limits.

Monga Waratah

It has the shape of an open hand that reaches out, therefore it helps the person to find his own inner strength that allows him to act freely. I'm people incapable Of Do the what's this from alone And they constantly need others. Tendency to download on others their commitments. For easily addicted people, who don't yes they feel never "up to" And that not they succeed to express yourself.
It can help people find their inner strength that will allow Of Act freely. Free from Everything is fine guy Of addiction from people And behaviors.

- It helps to strengthen the awareness of relying primarily on themselves. Neutralize situations that make you feel oppressed or suffocate in relations that not yes has the courage or not yes owns the force Of truncate.

It's one essence that strengthens there own will.
For problems related to the loss of personal power, to need of the other And at the addiction from they.
The person is afraid of not being able to do it alone, fears not to be strong enough, to need the help of others to to go forward.
The remedy helps to recover one's spirit, to find strength inner And to close relations insane.

Mountain Devil

The name Mountain Devil derives from the particular fruit it presents two bumps, which they remember there head of the devil.
The red of the flowers indicates the intensity of the emotions. The seven flowers symbolize spirituality since this number represents the learning Of a lesson Of which, naturally, there more important is the expression of love.
The sharp leaves, on the other hand, are like sharp words that they hold the other to mind inflicting ache.
The fruit, with the two protuberances, resembles the head of devil.
To be released, seeds often need fire destroys the slag to reveal the core. Winged seeds are like the angels that I am escaped to the fire of hell. THE fruits they remain on the tree for years, how the old grudges And the resentment that require a fire purifier for to be eliminated. People who react with feelings of bitterness e wish of revenge if they hear that I am be hurt and offenses.
They have great difficulty in relationships and expressing their own love, for this not they know to say what's this agreeable or to be lovely. Cautious, selfish, competitive and distrustful personalities, but many times this aggression it serves for conceal And defend yourself from a deep sadness they can't bear to admit to conscious level. Generally self-centered, they ask and demand from others as if they were obliged to give, e they may react violently to frustration. hate a other is equivalent to hating oneself; what we think of others is what we are thinking of ourselves even though we are not we want accept, for this reason the other there it serves from mirror. Obviously it is easier to project our shortcomings and inability in those around us, and not seeing it in ourselves. Normally they have a big tendency to accidents, not for cause from the clumsiness or of acceleration, but for the self-destruction.
There predominance Of these emotions negative does Yup that notthey reach easily there sensation Of "happiness".

They must learn to forgive and love, rejoice in happiness of the other And be able to to share.
The essence develop the generosity, the give And the to share.
Awaken there part improve Of each one.
Allows Of to enjoy of love.
AND' the remedy more important for there lack Of love.
Allows Of connect with the love unconditional, And with the possibility of the pardon.

- Needs to be used in everyone the States emotional where is it yes perceives lack of love, in its various manifestations. Love is the most important force in life, and all evolution human is based on our ability to express more and more amount of love. Negative states that indicate lack of love are hate, jealousy, anger and suspicion, emotions that yes they see daily and that this essence deals with.

The essence free And cleans hate, anger And other emotions that there they block. But doing this "cleaning", can to appear a deep sadness that is the reflection of that lack of love towards we themselves that simultaneously hinders the our love towards others. This remedy is very suitable for people that they stand crossing a separation in which there is a lot of hate and manipulation and for children when a is born little brother or a little sister.

Mulla Mulla

This remedy is for those people who have had experiences traumatic with the fire, how Being burned to cause Of a fire or hot objects. These people feel apprehension or afraid of fire or heat, and have difficulty with tools domestic how reeds chimneys, ovens, stoves. Can to be necessary to prepare a cream or gel with the essence to be applied locally. The effect Of this essence on sunburn is spectacular.

The fear of heat and fire is often unconscious and can manifest with a lack of vitality, as it happens during the summer period, when it is very hot and there is very sultry.

Whenever there is a burning sensation in the body, it is good to think of Mulla Mulla, as in the case of vaginitis, eczema or hot flashes Of heat in menopause.

- Work a lot well in the cases Of temperature high, lowering it.

Children commonly have a fever when they are ill and Mulla Mulla relieves fear caused by high temperature. There fever exhausts the child and this causes him fear; such fear steal oxygen to the body inhibiting further there capacity Of check the state feverish.

- Another feature of this Essence is to protect from radiation. Protects from the negative action of the rays ultraviolet products for there destruction from the cooker hood Ofozone. It also helps to repel any static electricity that builds up absorbs during a flight and which causes a decrease in potassium, oxygen And water in cells.

Useful also in the cases Of problems at the skin that they get worse self thereperson yes exhibits to the Sun And, logically in case of sunburn.

For people intolerant to heat and sun, especially in summer.

IS state also used in people that they manifest heaviness in legs, when does very hot.

In very severe burns, even Of 3rd degree, Mulla Mulla essence was used with the result to avoid plastics skin.
In 1st and 2nd degree burns it helps relieve pain and already the day after the skin no longer shows any signs, even with the sunburn caused from boiling water or for exposure solar.

63

Old Man Banksia

Remedy for sad people, who often have low energy and which they are slow in movement and extremely lazy.
I'm discouraged, tired, sluggish, indolent And often they suffer Of a activities thyroid slowed down. But they hide the They fatigue And they struggle with one effort incessant.
They are great listeners, love to help others and never know to say no. They are people with considerable common sense who do not they do nothing in a hurry, they are practical, methodical and very patient e available. The flower helps to deal with any life situation presents And to recognize the own limits giving the courage Of to say no. For generous people who love the hearth can't refuse requests from friends and family by exceeding i own limits physical and emotional. Of usual they prefer a clothing that not accentuate the forms or there sensuality in public because they don't want to be the center of attention.

- This remedy associates with the slow-thinking and slow-thinking personality type in action, low in energy and lacking in passion for life. Ian White says that: "They are more earthly in nature, as if the gravity exerted more influence on them. For this reason they operate better in the plan physicist or emotional, more that in the mental."

They have a to walk slow And heavy, how self drag their feet and always seem to be tired, or debilitated for some event.
They are people who are very fond of the family and in many cases they assume the load And there responsibility Of this.
They relate excellently with children, are very intuitive and they enjoy this cheerfulness. They like the contact with nature and they generally prefer the mountain climate. They know how to listen big and children, they are patient, generous and methodical.

Paw Paw

When a person is in difficulty in the take the greater decisions from the life, strengthens the process intuitive, helping to find solutions to problems without feeling overwhelmed by responsibility. Donate there capacity Of to focus the problem, lucidity and clarity. Useful when a person has been exposed to a lot of information or new ideas tiring from assimilate.

It is, therefore, suitable for students especially in the period of exams, or for those who find themselves short on time for study and end up discouraged without even starting. Paw Paw solves this situation and helps to fulfill the former step.

Paw Paw is such an intense remedy that it is possible take it in single doses whenever a student, or anyone else in a similar situation, please hear it overwhelmed or in difficulty to to integrate the information new.

- It is indicated before or after a seminar or conference for assimilate the knowledge.
- On a character level it is useful for those people who feel downtrodden, unable to solve problems and fall easilyin paintings of prostration and exhaustion.

Reorient And from there direction when must take a decision and relieves emotional tension. It's such a remedyintense, that it is possible to take it in single doses whenever a person finds himself in the difficult situation of having to integrate new information. It is indicated, for example, before or after a seminar to assimilate the new material. Physically yes combine well with Crowea for everyone the disturbances digestives, abs and of bad absorption.

Peach Flower Tea Tree

It is the remedy for those who lack the will to continue something they initially had great enthusiasm for and that Now there has left without interest. Those who I am subjects to swings in a mood, to fluctuating moods and hypochondria.
The flower it helps to find a renewed equilibrium.

- It increases accountability for the own health And stimulates the will to complete projects of is lost interest quickly by helping to develop constancy, consistency And to find the right reasons.

Being people rapids in acquiring any what in short term, they become overwhelmed with boredom and therefore give up the project. A appearance positive Of this essence is given come on balances emotional, from the confidence with self themselves, from the ability to achieve goals by taking responsibility for one's health without being distressed about it, while usually people who need this essence lose a lot weather and energies, yes they depress Of forehead at the own inconsistency And yes they feel frustrated front to Everything is fine lost. People who easily lose interest in an activity or a project after who started it.
They have difficulty to stabilize the own emotions, so long as theremoods always dominate iridescent and extremes.
When I'm in a bad mood they are aggressive and sharp with the other. Monotonous, boring, lacking in common sense, unwilling and fearful of the diseases.
They have fear from the old age, of pollution, Ofget intoxicated or get infected if they visit a sick.
In general they waste their own energy and time and this leads them to always miss opportunities, reason for the which yes they depress And they get frustrated.

- The flower provides at the stability physics And psychic.

Develop the willpower to get there without apologizing with fears. The emotions dominant in this flower I am: frustration, despondency, depression, lack of enthusiasm, boredom, fear of physical deterioration, inability to express e assimilate love or dominate the hate.
Peach Flowered Tea tree is a balancing of the pancreas also for insulin addictions.

- The Positives of Peach Flowered Tea Tree are emotional balance, self-confidence, the ability to achieve goals, as well as take responsibility from the own health, without excessive worries.

Philoteca

This quality is important for understanding the main feature Of this essence in how much it helps there people to accept the recognition of the others on They capacity and successes.
Erase the compliments or praise he receives, reject them or he does not feel worthy to receive them. There is an unconscious sense of guilt that forces them to give up those praises. Not can recognize And accept the They characteristics positive. He is often generous, selfless, as well as good listener, but has difficulty recognizing himself, for example, accept compliments from others and it tends to shy.
It is important that we consider the objectives and accept also recognition for our achievements, because it helps us stay in touch with our projects and the goals we set for them turn there they will allow to reach the purposes of life.
These people give too much of themselves, they listen carefully to others other's are shy, do not trust and do not accept recognition and praise. They are conditioned from an early age not to have successful, because they subconsciously feel that they would have to pay to dear price for this.
Moreover they feel to invade easily the space personal And this is lived how a danger. Generally I am fatalists And they accept the They destiny without fight.

Pink Flannel Flower

Its essence allows us to be grateful for all aspects from the life and for what that we experience environment around us.

- It gives us the opportunity to appreciate and enjoy every moment of the little things in life in awareness of one's own precious existence.

Otherwise there life could easily become boring, deprive Of color, flat with there result lost from the "joy Of to live".
Understanding is the door to fulfillment and peace and this essence can help us understand and appreciate when events arrive unexpectedly and will allow us to see the situation through a lens that gives us the ability to evaluate things from another one angle And not alone through there anger and the judgment.

Pink Mulla Mulla

For those that they have right away a wound spiritual deep And old, the result of some trauma, which left an old woman scar in soul and psyche. The flower helps to solve the original trauma beyond the state of consciousness. People who yes they close in a hedgehog to keep others at a distance. They are isolated and lonely.

In past yes I am feel denigrated, wounded or treated unfairly and they were deeply influenced by it, so much to appear deeply wounded, therefore in relationships with others they are suspicious.

Dominated by a strong fear of being hurt, they develop a reactive behavior: they become painful, acidic and critics.

This leads them to have many relationship problems with the They way Of express yourself and confront with the people.

They hide their feelings of insecurity and fear ofto be wounded, covering them with language offensive And aggressive.

Often they have prejudices And I am very insecure.

- There function Of this essence is to provide safety, receptivity, without fear Of to be invaded or wounded.

While Southern Cross yes self pity without take on there responsibility of the own actions, Pink Mulla Mulla tends to protect yourself from the possibility of be abused or exploited.

The Essence it helps to have trust, to open And to to interact morefreely.

Red Grevillea

It is a very powerful remedy for those people who feel blocked, trapped as in a spider's web, addicted to something or from someone.
From force in walking away from situations negative.
I'm people hypersensitive, that yes they do condition give her criticism and unpleasant people. It is a useful remedy when there yes find in a situation that yes wants change, because yes haswell in mind what would be better, but not self it has the courage.
The flower helps to find the strength to leave behind situations unpleasant And the audacity in undertaking finally there own Street.
It makes you indifferent to the judgments of others and independent psychologically and brave.
These individuals feel that they cannot advance and maintain a project with will, poise or enthusiasm and they lose strength and courage to continue.
Generally yes they associate to other people because in this manner yes they assure there continuity of the task, although there most of the time they do it in a destructive way or with whomthey don't have to. They feel blocked by invisible strings that hold them they bond with people or situations and are generally very sensitive at criticisms. This there does suffer And to tend to shut up insidethemselves until each day costs them more to get out of their shells where is it yes take refuge. Many times this there does to appear how unpleasant And grumpy in They relations. They have clear the goal towards which they wish to go, but in fact for them they are hard to reach goals, since all that means change or transformation is a big obstacle. The function of the flower is to promote independence, face challenges, push forward, to be constants And discover which is there Street correcttowards the goals.
The lesson this flower teaches us is to learn to to be independent And have courage.

Red Helmet Orchid

Red Helmet Orchid is a plant dwarf with a single leaf heart-shaped that grows on the flower.
This orchid has there characteristic Of to help the fathers to relate to the children, eliminating tiredness mental due to too work for be able to like this arrange Of more Attention in the report.

- It's useful also for the children when there I am problems unresolved with the father (even if deceased or very old) or for those people who are rebellious and have problems towards of the authority And from the law.

The flower favors the link father/son, in the discovery of a renewed form of sensitivity andrespect.

Red Lily

The red lily is a perennial aquatic plant that comes from a rhizome creeping underwater. It grows in swamps temporary of the floodplains in the Top End of Australia.

- The remedy Red Lily it helps to balance the plan spiritual And the earthly one. It keeps people with i feet for earth, preserving the sense practical And, in same time, allows them to rise up to touch the realms spiritual.

Incorporates the properties of Aboriginal spirituality australians, a spirituality a lot loud And rooted.
The look negative of the remedy is represented give it individuals who do not they place on plan ground.
They do not have any interest for the events worldly And for the here I'm, And They tend to fantasize And to live in future.
Often these people they have one gaze new detached, distant. Generally they live in a condition unhappy And, therefore, they flee to a fantasy world, where they dream situations different. Red Lily people often have poor concentration because their mind is elsewhere. They are very distracted and lack sense practical; they live through the thought rather that the action. They have few memories, because they don't lend Attention to the events happening around them. It's frustrating to have a conversation with these people, because they don't really listen to what is being said to them He says; they often interrupt by going off on a tangent. Level physicist tend to be rather clumsy because they do not lend be careful what they do, and they may be victims of repeated accidents.

- They sleep a lot, another form of escape, and can be attracted give her drugs, in particular the hallucinogenic.

IS a optimal remedy for those that they have difficulty to to focus And to start work coping the practical tasks.

Red Suva Frangipani

This essence is addressed to emotions of great intensity, difficulty And adversity in the case Of a relation that is crossing a period particularly hard or that is finished.
It is specific for relational moments marked by greatness difficulty And intense coldness.

- The flower give renewed calm And satisfaction.

It helps to find peace interior and the calm for face the difficulty. When there is intense and immediate pain and agitationfaced with the threat or reality that the loved one is in it leaving, to part or why is dying.
For the people that during there break up Of a relation or in moments of turmoil feel very fragile and grieving and they cry often.
For the great emotional intensity, the pain, the sadness and the upheaval that the people can try when a relation is finishing or is crossing a period stormy.

Rough Bluebell

This essence helps people express love fully inherent in themselves and to teach them to love and exploit their own potential. Does to express unconditional love.
AND' also indicated for people that they hurt, they manipulate And they deliberately exploit their neighbor, for the malicious, for those which they are strongly centered on self themselves.
The flower give compassion and sensitivity towards the other.
Free the vibrations of love, helping the individual to express themcompletely, develop empathy
I'm people that they do use manipulative Of other people. They have a great capacity Of feel the weaknesses of the other. I'm inclined to greed moral and manipulations psychopaths.

- The function of this essence is to liberate the object of the gods own wishes aggressive, Of domain And Of hate from theown personality.

In the clinic it can be used to release toxins, treat irritations from the skin, for people perverse And cruel.

She Oak

There greatest function of the remedy is related to the factors emotional that they inhibit the fertility of woman.

- It is of benefit for those women that they have problematic to become pregnant, despite not having physical pathologies. Also useful for women that they have syndrome premenstrual or cycles irregular orIn the period from the menopause.
- Has dosages different respect at various problematic.

This essence describes a person that has of the imbalances in wait feminine.

I'm women that generally they tend to cover up or to hide their feminine aspects, their ability to seduction, the They shapes physical.

Often they have had problems in the relationship with theirs mother And there maternity it becomes a compromise difficult from face up to. If they have daughters, they have issues with the latter and have difficulty understanding them and often a issue of competitiveness.

Another important trait is a lack of confidence in abilities creative that a woman can have and this emotional block yes posters with infertility, such as the inability to conceive, too if not there are causes known for that is.

It is very useful in women who feel incompetent and fearful at first son.

- The essence is also very useful in cases where a conflict indoor united to a loud fear unconscious towards the pleasure sexual And there dresser Of to be a person unworthy, generates feelings of shame and guilt that they hinder there freedom necessary for to reach the orgasm. The uterus is the matrix it represents in the body the identity feminine and his capacity creative.

problems, confusions And malfunctions in this area indicate

the presence of conflicts with being a woman who have an intimate relation with the own lived from the femininity.

In the case of men She Oak works on, insecurities, and doubts compared to the male condition and the fear of losing the manhood.

She oak is also useful for there retention water that characterizes the cycle menstrual, And how therapy substitute hormonal in the menopause.

Silver Princess

The essence is indicated for those who they are insecure of the own life plan or purpose. Many people aren't actually at knowledge of the plan business suit from the own existence, but they let that come revealed during from the itself.

- Silver Princess can be hired when they come to a crossroads either at a turn and are not sure of the next step. In these moments not they have a objective or a direction clear.

The feeling of doing the right thing, really necessary for its own existence is extremely rewarding.

When you have no purpose, you feel frustrated or demoralized. Some people they become aware Of that is that they want Do only very late when is difficult make the changes necessary. However, self they have reached up truly this awareness and they are determined I respect them own choices, the what's this yes they put inevitably to place And yes present the right opportunity. Another role of Silver Princess is that of helping to find a new direction after that they have reached up a objective significant.

When people are focused on an important goal, often ignore the daily aspects of life, so when they reach the purpose they tend to say: "is that all?"

Silver Princess serves to appreciate the path to the own objective And, a turn reached up, to find the motivations for pursue one new.

Goals are very important and it is very important to have them, many times the benefits to they related not I am those that we imagined. Many times the effect he arrives enough quickly, but usually it is necessary to take the essences forperiods a bit' more long respect the normal two weeks.

Slender Rice Flower

This essence it helps to bring in a group harmony And cooperation and to overcome ideologies such as racism and remedy at the scarce availability that can occur inside of Of a union of any kind, to allow one to see the different ones facets of an issue or situation: both sides of the medal. The flower gives the discovery of cooperation and of harmony Of group, there perception from the beauty of the other.
It helps to learn to accept the other, in a understanding universal. I'm people that they do comparisons, expressing prejudices and the essence helps Do understand that nobody is in the position Of be able to to judge another person or another group, stimulates to recognize there beauty in whoever And anything.

- Moreover favors humility, part integral Of a greater understanding capacity that brings harmony and cooperation between people, while pride And envy neither indicate there lack.

Donate tolerance, flexibility, wish Of I listen active, collaboration for the common good. These kind of people are very rigid in They ideas And beliefs.
I'm proud, arrogant, jealous And little inclined at the cooperation. They let themselves be guided by prejudices and starting from they disqualify everything they deem not suitable, whether people or ideas. They judge food habits harshly, how the consumption Of meat, alcohol, there cigarette or whatever behavior that not mirror the their values.
The essence floral sign to to share And respect the differences. This state marks a strong presence of resentment, hate And intolerance, Of pride, suspected, And Of wish Of vengeance. Competitive And voracious, they prefer move inside an elite, scorning garlic other And they wish there perfection. Usefulin psychosis paranoid And in allergies.

Useful for the resentment And there mentality victimization.
There is a feeling that life has been very hard and unfair and of have never been rewarded for their efforts ("It's not right!").
They think they have no control over their lives e therefore they do not feel responsible for the creation of the own reality and tend to blame others, but never if themselves. They project their misfortunes onto others or into situations external.
They feel unjustly excluded, they show themselves as victims of circumstances. they ask in way constant a Help excessive.
They are immature, irresponsible and careless, with great difficulty look inside yourself. This leads them to blame others for to interfere in the own happiness. I'm hypercritical And pessimists.
They envy the successes others And the memberships materials.
cranky, frown, grumpy, they assume tones complaining And they wait for the world to provide for them, just because I am victims of circumstances beyond outside Of their control.
Also when not they regret directly the others, they believe however life is against them and they always expect the worse.
Recrimination for long weather for a deed Of injustice. Little will And effort personal.
Lack Of experience in the life. Resignation.
The feeling of being pushed and tossed by life accelerates definitely the aging process and this, associated to bitterness, can   affect also on organs interior, in especially the liver and gallbladder. The sense of resignation can Bring to a lack of power and of vitality.
The essence helps to get load Of self themselves.

Spinifex

Has a action Of cleaning. Can be , therefore, a optimal adjuvant in case of candidiasis, infections fungal and herpes.

It can be applied as a topical to the skin for acne and eczema. Taking the remedy by mouth, it helps stop the blisters on the surface emotions that they cause the blisters from the skin.

Emotional problems can then be resolved with essence floral appropriate.

For who to express the own ache, there shortage And there difficulty in the skin. I'm personality discreet that yestake refuge inside the own body, not show the feelings, fear the bodily closeness of others e they have some kind of body armor that makes them take distance. It is not a character remedy, but it clarifies there emotional cause that gave rise to the annoyances and of which the individual suffers.

The emotions that Of usual yes they hide in this essence can to be shame, devaluation, rejection, vulnerability, irritation, annoyance, excitement sexual suffocated.

The specific action that this essence has on the skin makes us think that the people Spinifex think that the other the they can seefor their own insecurities and uncertainties. The skin is a screen of projection of our internal world that we do not express.

- For the topical applications, it is useful to dilute seven drops of essence with a some clean water and apply a wet patch to the wound, or spray the water directly on the wound; the application it goes repeated morning And evening. IS possible to use the essence simultaneously at the level indoor and external.

When herpes blisters begin to develop, their development, this can be stopped by spraying the essence on affected area. In many cases, herpes is triggered by a sense ofguilt tied up at the sexuality, or from a abuse or trauma sexual, which can be alleviated by combining the remedy with Fringed Violet And Wisteria.

People suffering from herpes, for example, often feel victims of the disease. It appears repeatedly, without any reason evident, weakening the system immune And there safety of the individual, creating unease physicist or ache. Generally, the attacks are triggered by negative beliefs acquired in the first years Of life And keep in the subconscious. Many people yes they feel more strong when they understand that whatever happens on the physical plane comes from the emotional plane e that can change beliefs And attitudes that they determine the They conditions physical, inducing like this therehealing.

- Spinifex can to be employee also in the treatment of the Chlamydia infections, an organism that causes infections in the throat, as well as to the stretch urinary And to the system reproductive.

Sturt Desert Pea

It's indicated for wounds deep keep in mind from many years.
It is the essence for deep trauma, sadness and suffering a emotional level. The flower frees from sad memories and gives a renewed motivation And force for to go forward. People who have a very great pain in their hearts and the they keep from very weather, without be able to to solve. Old pains how wounds that not I am heal, usually caused by the loss of a loved one. When faced with suffering, they internalize it and cry in silence. Frequently, the accumulation Of emotions not elaborate they deviate in pathologies corporal, especially respiratory And pulmonary.
On an emotional level, they have the feeling that it is no longer possible do nothing, that no one can help them a feeling of some what of irreparable, impossible to to solve.
They have difficulty asking for help. sorry, depression, ache psychic.

- It is a flower that acts very quickly, it helps in the depression, meloncholy, distress acute, the ache current or old emotional that no longer has tears. It helps to disperse the memories sad Of distant pains And old wounds.

Sturt Desert Rose

Essence helps people follow their beliefs and moral principles, as well as doing what they know they should do: give to the individual there force to be loyal to itself same.

Guilt can lead to self-criticism and constant searching of the mistake, generating an oppression general in the individual. Often they establish models very elevated for self themselves, meeting then difficulty to live accordance with to those royaltiesand feeling, of consequence, inadequate And guilty.

- This remedy gives the strength to be honest with yourself and it can be used whenever a person feels guilty about something that has happened, even if he is not responsible for it attributable. The wait positive Of this remedy I am a increased sense of the own convictions And from the own integrity personal.

You do what you know you have to do and you accept what happened in the past, succeeding like this to to go forward.

Sturt Desert Rose is the remedy for there guilt, it helps the people to follow his internal beliefs and do that that they have to Do, and being be honest with them themselves.

It is also very important to improve one's self-esteem a person that it turns out to be low how consequenceof past actions for a form of remorse for what it was done in the past, or for that that not it was done.

Remorse hinders people from enjoying all the things in lifecan offer them. These personalities normally ask for apologies for all; but they may also believe that others are talking always hurting them or criticizing them, since that's what they do with themselves everything the weather.

Everything is fine turn that It happens something yes they feel responsible. They take heavy loads upon them: obligation and duty are there most important thing. These feelings are stimulated by various what's this how the education rigid, the sent cultural And the religions.

For those who can't get rid of remorse for a past action that the does to hear devalued.

Guilt may not be enough clear in the consciousness of the individual, but equally produces a emotional block and there lack of self esteem.

There her origin can to be in childhood, in the relation with the own parents that generally they appear how suffocating, critical, blaming. They can also be unwanted children or abandoned. Generally yes they feel inadequate, how self no place or possibility could to go well because not they think they be deserving of the what's this good from life.

IS very typical that, self some person nearby dies, there personality Sturt Desert Rose curtain to blame yourself for the what's this thathe thought, He has not said and not has made for that person.

Sundew

Versus the indecision, there trend to postpone, there lack Of concentration. I am vague and indecisive person, know online general how to perform a task, but fail to pose Attention to the details. I'm emotionally fought, especially if they have to do some what Of not pleasant.

Daydreamers. The flower brings out the practical sense, attention for the details, there concentration And there precision.

- It is indicated for the sense Of indeterminacy, dissociation and dissolution of the self which becomes a way to alienate from situations of life.

Some people can mask a resentment level very deep, resentful of the fact that others do not pose a lot of attention, and therefore end up taking refuge in their own ideas and beliefs, finding them much more interesting than what happening outside and forgetting everything that happens in the world external. This flower has a effect anchor, carrying to accept there reality, centering the existence And bringing her back under control. Sundew personalities lack determination and I am excessively dreamers. sentimental, romantics, little realistic And little practical. Generally undecided, with scarce attention span and not very precise. There stop the details. By hand the what's this unknown, esoteric, spiritual.

They are passionate about science fiction, meditation practices, to viewing. They use this mode to call back attention and to be treated like something special.

I'm hindered from the Do, from the what concrete And they tend to postpone to tomorrow.

They dissociate easily. Introverts, they find the most interesting wire of their own thoughts that the refer with the other.

Sunshine Wattle

To survive long periods of drought and the Australian climate rugged and arid, most acacias have no true trees leaves, but a developed leaf stalk. Sunshine Wattle is a shrub open that can to reach the 2 m Of height, come on flowers Ofa color gold pale. THE fluffy flower heads I am, in reality, bunches Of 6-15 little flowers with long stamens Detective stories containing lots of pollen. Its habitat is made up of the maquis of the areas arid And give her forests dry, come on slopes rocky from the ground poor.

It helps to accept and enjoy the beauty of the present, developing trust for the future And restoring the optimism.

For those that not they remember the past how a happy moment, they are still entangled in what is to him happened and they bring their own negative experiences too in the here I'm. Sensation Of have to always fight for earn something.

- The flower give optimism, hope. It helps to realize how beautiful and a source of joy the present that it becomes a pleasant one premise for the future.

Great remedy to take when life is temporarily difficult, seems to be a big battle or when nothing good seems to happen. The predominant emotions for the people who need this essence are: disappointment, lack of attachment to life, fatalism, discouragement, sadness, lack Of cheerfulness, recollection, not affectivity, resignation, pessimism. There lesson that needs to learn is that Of accept that the life not is linear, but has tall and bass.

Must learn to believe in the future.

Sensation Of to be to pieces And psychologically destroyed, Of being alienated and unloved by others. Conviction of being abnormal and alone.

- The flower gives the ability to realize who we are all unique and therefore special people. Feeling of safety and of peace. Discovery Of a communication sincere.

Tall Mulla Mulla

They are rather labile personalities, willing to support what they give other they want feel to say. By hand the what's this pleasant, while they feel aversion to conflicts, disharmony and confrontations with the others. Fear of going out and interacting with others, refusal to mingle with more people. Tendency to prefer solitary life own out of fear of the comparison.

- The flower helps to feel comfortable and secure in the midst of other people.
- Encourage the relations social.

For the wish Of to maintain there calm can also to be agree or say things they don't really believe. Often they say what they think people want to hear. When I with the people they have a loud wish Of to remain in harmony.

They have a big aversion to the conflict, at the disharmony And especially to clashes and confrontation for this as soon as they can, they seek Of to run away, for the fear that these what's this they can to happen. They don't like mixing with people because they feel very uncomfortable, and insecure, and in danger, so they forgive the opportunity to grow emotionally through interaction with the others. They don't live life fully, because they prefer sticking to what is familiar, rather than opening up to the new. There is no detachment And coldness in they.

They just want to live without the fuss and fuss, in the belief that is impossible have quiet self yes is between other people.

Tall Mulla Mulla turns out to be an extreme remedy help with asthma attacks. Precisely in this pathology it will be useful to add: Crowea for muscle spasms, Flannel Flower to relieve suffocating emotions, Sturt Desert Rose for the ache And there sadness, emotion typically connected to the lungs.

Tall Yellow Top

Sense of alienation, loneliness and isolation characterized by a lack Of connection or Of sense Of membership to anything like family, a job or a reality social or national. They are people who feel such an emptiness big at heart to have cut with their feelings in order to suppress the ache And like this doing they live, taking refuge exclusively in their heads. This mode has been ported forward for long weather And to times all a life.
The essence helps to reconnect the cognitive sphere to that emotional, give there rediscovered from the sensation Ofbelong to a group (family, friends, Colleagues Ofwork), and favors the relations with the other.

- AND' an essence from to use for long weather until to 6-8 weeks without interruptions And, self necessary, needs to repeat at same way.

It is possible that the issues of belonging and isolation are due to experiences that took place at a very young age, such as a abandonment or parents that not they have desired the son duringthe pregnancy. Useful in all cases where there is a sense of not belonging, of rejection by others and in cases where there is a lack of the sense Of "home". For those depressions Of people that for to bear the ache And be able to go forward, they suppress the They feelings And yes islander in solitude. Very useful in families disunited or in Which not there is containment affective. For people who strongly identify with the own work and when they lose it they fall into a feeling of alienation And low self esteem.

Turkey Bush

This essence favors the expression from the own creativity. For those with creative blocks due to loss of self-confidence capacity.
The flower give inspiration, creativity, it helps the people to tune in on its own creativity And to express it. .
Renew there trust in own capacity artistic.

- It is the essence for artists, creators who feel without inspiration.

For people who are ashamed to express or shape their own ideas or distrust of They capacity creative.
Children that they destroy the own drawings And teenagers that they hide i their writings, poems, paintings.
For who judge hard the own expressions artistic, wanting find there perfection And not the pleasure.
I'm people excessively rational, with little imagination, repressed out of shame, fear, aridity.
It is an essence that is useful for initiating and developing possibilities creative that I am latent in all the people. For to enjoy Of everything that you create, or that others create or that was created by same nature.

- Turkey Bush is extremely useful associated with She Oak to treat infertility problems where infertility can hide an inability to "procreate".

Waratah

It is the remedy that helps to have courage or to raise its level.
For there deep despair, there lost Of Everything is fine hope, the inability to react to crises. The flower gives tenacity, confidence, ability to adaptation And of survival.
In state emotional Waratah, the individual yes find in a situation that lives as hopeless and in which (in real form or imaginary) is in I play the her survival.
The person feels that he lacks ability or courage for face it And to solve there crisis in the which yes hear trapped. The pressure of the circumstances in which he finds himself makes him that lose there vision Of together of the what's this or have a confused and cloudy perception, as if there were a veil that prevents Of see with clarity. In same weather there is uncertainty, instability And yes is inclined to to react in manner inadequate in the face of external stimuli.

- This remedy is used in crisis situations, catastrophes, traumas, panic, anguish, hysteria, lost of the control. For exceed emotional blocks, big challenges, to face, states of exhaustion with the feeling of notto be able to to to go forward or to be condemned for the life.
- Moreover is a useful remedy for people with ideas, conducted or trends suicide.

At your place the conditions treated with this remedy, is necessary that it act very quickly.
THE benefits initials I am immediate And in many cases the full effects are achieved in a short time, sometimes they are sufficient from 5 to 7 days.

Wedding Bush

For people who have a hard time committing to relationships with others, in employment, in the family or even in the own goals personal.

Often, it seems that these individuals flee from self themselves, avoiding Everything is fine responsibility. So is a optimal remedy from take when starting a company or any other form of bond or collaboration. In any activity or regime that requires discipline And I commit (diets slimming, sports).

- Useful when in the couple the physical attraction of the former period passes and there is a decline in interest within from the couple. Self the partner they wish to engage again one in the comparisons of the other, or when a individual wants stop Of to pass from a relation to the other.

They are emotionally unstable people, and prone to surfacing soon boredom in relationships. Everything for them is transient, so don'tthey have continuity in the projects they undertake. I do not want to lose nothing, but actually over time they forgive everything.

Another one characteristic important is that they have a low frustration tolerance, emotionally fickle, attraction initial fades, they are afraid of responsibility and lack of will beyond to have fear to be love yourself.

It can also be excellent for those who become parents by offering the ability to engage in this task by preparing it with joy.

Wild Potato Bush

It is the remedy indicated for those who are not in harmony with the own physical body. Often these people feel the need to to go to the Of there of the own limitations physical, how self the body there held And there oppressed. For there sensation Of oppression And of being imprisoned in a personality that does not belong to us more.
It is an essence addressed to the frustration of limitation. Donate a sense Of vitality and Of freedom Of change into life.

- Useful for the women during the last one period from the pregnancy and for people who have physical disabilities. Also useful for children in their first years of life feel frustrated because of the lack of control they haveof your own body.

Can to be also used for those people that I am in overweight, due to a sense of inadequacy that leads them to use the their fat how coverage.
In all diseases in which there is frustration due to diminished functionality physics, it helps to accept the limitations of the body physicist. These people they feel a loud weight on They shoulders.
There tiredness, the sorry And there depression there they exhaust.
They have a slow heavy walk as if the body were one prison that imprisons them, a heavy bag that nullifies theirs movements. Generally they have been strong people of character, but suffering has robbed them of their energy source and diminished their energy their vitality. The face reveals the pain suffered, they have a look shady And won, with there head reclined, how self not they now wished to see ahead, as if the future did not existed and wanted to get rid of that dejected body and too much load, for give place at the regeneration. The emotions that related to this flower are: frustration, restrictions, feelings of oppression, tiredness And sadness.

Wisteria

This remedy is aimed primarily at women, but it can be also used by men who prefer to flaunt an image from macho, denying the own appearance real.
The flower allows you to agree to have a kinder side and nice. For women that not yes they feel to own comfortable with there own sensuality. Discomfort for one's physicality as a result of past sexual abuse.

- The remedy gives self-confidence and in the own partner. Satisfaction And pleasure in the own life sexual. It helps to break up to go, permitting at own sensations of express yourself.
- Wisteria hired with Fringed Violet dissolves blocks emotional.

Many genital and reproductive problems are the reflex Of related issues to the sex.
In many cultures women are instilled from childhood mistaken beliefs that hinder a right expression of femininity. Wisteria give trust in self themselves And in the own partner, satisfaction and pleasure in sex, helps to let go allowing your feelings to express themselves freely. Very useful in the gynecological problems.

Yellow Cowslip Orchid

I'm people that they address the own energies mostly to the intellect, much that often they block the own feelings.
This imbalance leads to criticizing and judging and being extremely bureaucratic And skeptical and exaggeratedly cautious in accepting the what's this.

- It is the flower linked to the pituitary gland; balances the pituitary primarily for women that they have hired the pill for many years.

Donate interest for the problems of the next.
Develop impartiality, there capacity Of recognize the details Andthe objectivity in analyses generals, opening mental, skills to understand quickly the concepts. These personality I am excessively rational And analytical. For They there what more important is the intellect; the rest is secondary And so not justifies no concern. They are obsessive, scrupulous and yesthey block on little things. They are fond of rules and order, they observe the other people, with Do critic.
They are skeptical, irritable, suspicious and cautious; they don't like confrontation,but they prefer take the distances.
I'm naturally social, charismatic, And they know capture quickly le need of the other.
They have to learn to accept the ideas And the people, without criticism. The They world emotional is colored with L' irritability, there pettiness, irony, partiality, bad mood, irascibility, the coldness, acidity, detachment And caution in dialogue.

Blends Of Flowers Australians

For face up to specific States emotional, psychological And physical I am blends containing specific essences have been designed and formulated floral Australian that in the They usage joint is state verified to have a synergistic action aimed at the resolution of inconvenience physical, emotional And psychological encountered in determined situations. They are already diluted, they can be taken directly. Of following we highlight the blends related at main problematic.
The insights that they follow make simple identifythe suitable remedy to a particular circumstance.
The treatment normal expects a duration Of about a month.

- It is absolutely not recommended to use more than one remedy for time, with the exception of the Emergency and Stress Stop remedies which can be used in particular moments of stress or need, together with other Essences.

Adol

This essence was born to face all those problems that teenagers they commonly experience.
Favors the acceptance Of self themselves, there communication interpersonal, participation in social life, harmony in relations with the other, there maturity, there stability emotional And optimism, removing negative family conditioning, i lived Of grudge, the resentment, self-pity And there solitude. Favors the expression of the own feelings, of the own personal power and the implementation of a mental position suitable at own personality. Allows Of to live with trustand enthusiasm one of the steps more important from the life: adolescence. They come mixed together:

Billy goat Plum - mainly specific for the feelings of aversion or revulsion towards oneself, especially when they are addressed to organs or acts sexual. Also useful for skin problems, such as acne, eczema, psoriasis, herpes, warts, which contribute to cause a feeling of body "not clean".

Boab - eliminates family negative influences that are handed down Of generation in generation. Useful alsofor those people that they have right away abuse, persecutions or to whom prejudices have been handed down. It helps to break free from those family patterns acquired by rigidly favoring a personal growth positive and independent.

Bottlebrush - helps in maintaining a healthy and mutually beneficial relationship between mother and child. Excellent for teenagers that yes they feel submerged come on changes And give her evolutions more significant from the life, helping them to believe in own capacity Of face up to the new situations. It is supportive in all characterized moments by feelings of inadequacy, uncertainty and apprehension for the changes.

Daggers Hakea - it helps to tone down the emotions Of

resentment and anger, often experienced in this stage Of big changes, permitting the pardon And favoring the openness to the expressivity of feelings towards the family And the friends.

five Corners - allows Of to live the love Andthe acceptance of oneself, the celebration of one's own joy and beauty, replacing the lack of self-esteem, which is frequently felt in the moments of adversity And of great change, with love own.

flanner Flower - it helps to recognize and to express the own deepest feelings. It favors a greater sensitivity and kindness in physical contact and therefore, tooa greater approach to others, especially friends and people love.

Kangaroo Paw - helps teenagers to be more attentiveat need of the other, without to be exclusively absorbed from self themselves. Allows Of understand how Act appropriately in situations listening the suggestions from others. It allows you to enjoy and feel at own comfortable with other people that they have differentneeds And personality, with there awareness of the diversity, like this from transmit relaxation And understanding.

Red Helmet Orchid - it helps to create a report balanced And mutual between father And son; favors moreover the relationships between people who have difficulty with figures authoritarian or personality powerful. It helps to to recognize one's own personal abilities and to respect e consider those others.

Southern Cross - this essence is useful to people who they suffer Of self pity And that they feed there belief that life be lasts with They. Specific for the tendency to victimhood, promotes personal power, the positivity, awareness and empowerment for the happenings of the own life.

Sunshine Wattle - fosters optimism, expectations positive And the acceptance from the beauty And from the joy in the immediate present. Excellent for all who they live the life with excessive pessimism.

Tall Yellow Top – this essence is addressed at the trend depressive, to alienation And at the solitude, sensations often experience during the period adolescent, but also due to an estrangement from landmarks such as family, workplace or country. Restore there view Of self, of the world And of the own expectations futures.

To integrate with seven drops under there tongue, morning And evening.

Environment Purity

Environment Purity is suitable for get a environment balanced and harmonic, cleansed of negative energies. Create a harmonious environment ed balanced, freeing him from negative situations and allowing the people to live in a healthy and harmonious place. Very useful in environments frequented by many people, in places where they stay living moments difficult.
Used in whatever moment in Everything is fine place Closed givenew power positive it's a feeling of found Welfare.

angelsword : favors there understanding spiritual And renew communication with our deepest self. Helps eliminate negative psychic energies and bonds energetic excessive with others people.

Boab : Helps eliminate negative thought patterns resulting from family inheritance. Give personal freedom, often limited from beliefs And manifestations to emotional and mental character normally ingrained e transmitted by generation in generation.

fringed Violet : favors there protection general of the individual strengthening the field energetic or aura. Help shield us and remove the negative effects of fields electromagnetic or from the charge energy Of people that they tend to to invade the our space personal.

Lichen : helps to capture and enjoy positive energies emanate from the earth. It favors the acceptance of momentsof change.

Red lilly : favors a greater concreteness And concentration helping to live the present actively eliminating the feeling of having the "head in the clouds".However, it stimulates spiritual involvement in activities daily.
Vaporize often And Everything is fine turn self neither listen there needin the busy environment.

Concentration

Gives focus and clarity in any activity. Improve them ability to learn in study and work permitting the processing of new ideas And information.
Facilitates the contact with the own the in which I am enclosed all theknowledge And the experiences of the past And it helps to to balance the intuitive and cognitive mechanisms, integrating ideas and information. They come mixed together:

Bush Fuchsia - favors there communication interhemispheric cerebral, attenuating those difficulty of learning and expression that often derive from a marked lateralization functional.

Isopongo - makes the unconscious more accessible, allowing the recovery of removed skills and knowledge; it helps to recover the memories of the past emotionally loads And to to elaborate the experiences lived balanced.

Jacaranda - specific remedy to mitigate over- excitement: confers equilibrium, decision And clarity of thought, creating the ability to devise precise strategies and effective tools that allow you to complete each project with success.

Paw Paw - assimilation, integration and learning Of new ideas And information. Gets better access to the just it, with consequent recognition and reconquest of one's abilities to reduce any feelings of oppression. Very recommended during the period Of Preparation garlic exams.

Sundew - specific for there dissociation And so there depersonalization understood how defence from the reality to times bitter from the life. It helps to find there liveliness
of interest for the world external And the skill Of put also attention to detail, thus allowing you to take there right decision for Every single case.

To integrate with seven drops under there tongue, morning And evening.

Electro

Useful for shielding or reducing the negative effects of radiation which may cause irritability, mental numbness and disturbances of sleep. It is excellent for decreasing the negative effects of radiation electric issued from repeaters, mobile phones, computer, devices electronic how, to example, televisions, mobile phones, computer, favoring the achievement Of calm, Welfare Andvitality.
They come mixed together:

Bush Fuchsia - optimal for the people that they pass very weather Of forehead to a video, a computer or to devices electronic And that yes they feel a bit' numb to end day. It's simple to recognize this state Of weakness, in that trivial mistakes are made. This essence will dynamically reactivate the brain, eliminating the difficulty of learning, because accomplish with greater effectiveness the interconnection hemispherical cerebral. It helps to feel in harmony with the rhythms from thenature.

Crowea - has a powerful calming effect centered on body and mind, giving an intense sensation of Welfare And Of vitality. It helps to align the body ethericand astral with the physical body. Excellent for keeping a sense Of equilibrium psycho-physical when yes is to strict contact with radiation electromagnetic.

Fringet Violet - helps restore damaged aura. The aura can go up effects negatives from radiation electromagnetic, computer, repeaters. An aura not integrates can take away vitality And health.

Mulla Mulla - it helps to eliminate the radiation stored in the our body And to reduce the radiation electromagnetic absorbed from cell phones, computers, or other electronic devices. It is advisable take this essence immediately before each radiography or after each radiotherapy treatment, in how much it helps to reduce the negative effects of radiation absorbed.

Paw Paw - eases the feeling of being overwhelmed and overworked from a excess Of stimuli, favoring the assimilation And the integration Of ideas And informationhighlights. Donate a sense Of calm and clarity mental.

Waratah - promotes courage, tenacity, adaptability And there capacity Of resistence. This essence acts quickly And from courage in the exceed the crisis, the emergencies or big challenges.

To integrate with seven drops under there tongue, morning And evening.

Emergency

It has an immediate calming effect on the mind, body and legs emotions, too during the crisis of serious entity.

This combination is especially suitable for feelings of fear, panic, for serious stress mental And physical, voltage nervous And ache. Self is necessary a intervention doctor specific, it becomes a valuable remedy Of emergency until to when the treatment will not be available. The utility of this combination covers varied needs, that they range from anxiety pre-exam, to significant damage physical.

They come mixed together:

Angelsword - favors the find from the Truth Spiritual And from the Peace, helping to rediscover the values internalized in the past. Allows the contact with the our I more deep.

Crowea - gives balance and focus to the individual, relaxes muscles, relieves worries and stress. Donate peace, calm And force, promoting a sense OfWelfare And vitality.

dog Rose of wild Forces - it helps to check the emotions, so that those more intense not overwhelm the individual causing him to lose touch with reality e with if same.

Fringed Violet - "wipes away" the negative effects of concern for the present and the past, so that from to protect there fragility from the psyche in delicate breakers.

Gray Spider Flower - Specific essence for fears extremes, immobilizing panic and pervading terrorsuddenly.

It helps with other anxiety disorders, such as phobias and i disturbances psycho physiological with basis psychological, how asthma. It helps to acquire confidence, calmness and courage.

Sundew - specific for there dissociation And, so, there

depersonalization, understood how defence from the reality to times bitter from the life. It helps to find there liveliness of interest for the world external And the skill Of put also attention to detail, thus allowing you to take there right decision for Every single case.

Waratah - courage, tenacity, trust. Capacity Ofadaptation And survival.

Supplement with seven drops under the tongue every hour; in urgent cases also take seven drops every ten to fifteen minutes, until achieving some relief or until it does the intervention doctor. Through such intervention flower therapy, Emergency can to be hired for 15 days, facilitating the elimination Of States emotional limiting how there fear And anxiety.

Energy

Specific for people who don't feel fit and who are experiencing a situation of energy decline, sometimes accompanied from one state Of discouragement or exhaustion. Renew the enthusiasm And there joy for there life, favoring a greatest dynamicity.
They come mixed together:

Banksia Robur - specific remedy for people who they are usually dynamic and expressing their own enthusiasm vigorously, but that for determined reasons are tired, frustrated, or experiencing difficulties to to recover completely. It helps to remove there negativity that prevents there ascent to the Welfare.

Crowea - has a remarkable effect calming And invigorating on body and mind, giving an intense meaning of well-being and peace. It is a great remedy for anxiety that can remove power And vitality.

Illawara Flame Tree - helps take the first step for there concretization of the own potential, learning to listen to the aspirations of life, without feeling burdened with responsibilities. Balance the activity of the thymus, a gland of the immune system responsible for production of lymphocytes T.

Macrocarpa - optimal tonic physicist general, specific for the adrenal glands, which helps to strengthen health, making greater power. IS indicated in States Of weakening or strong exhaustion.

Old Man Banksia - specific remedy for people sad and plethoric who complain of little energy. It helps win back there power lost, rekindling there spark
of the force. Favors the balancing of the activity of the thyroid hormones.

Yellow Cowslip Orchid - favors the rebalancing energetic of the pituitary. Very useful for the people tend to be critical and judgmental. Help to cope the conflicts And the diversity with impartiality. It supports the activities celebrate them, favoring the integration of the new concepts And the opening towards the new ideas.

To integrate with seven drops under there tongue, morning And evening.

Equilibrium Woman

Women at any age are often found, due to their physiology natural, having to face situations of emotional imbalance. There puberty, the menstrual cycle but also childbirth, menopause are all conditions of physical change that cause situations difficult from exceed also from the point Of view emotional. There combination is so effective in the favor there calm And there stability, necessary for face up to the changes, as well as to become aware of one's inner and outer beauty. They come mixed together:

Billy Goat Plum - for feelings of shame and self- disgust. For every woman who perceives the sexual act with repulsion And repugnance. IS Of Help in skin problems such as, for example, acne, eczema anddermatitis especially when they are influenced by the cycle female hormone.

bottle brush - allows Of to live everyone the changes physical (pregnancy, menopause) and social with serenity e trust in the future. Favors a healthy And mutual report mother son.

Bush Fuchsia - favors the rebalancing of the hypothalamus e increases intuition and the ability to be in tune with the nature And the rhythms earthlings.

Crowea - has a remarkable effect calming And invigorating on body and mind, giving an intense meaning Of Welfare And quiet. IS a great remedy for anxiety.

Five Corners - promotes love and self-acceptance themselves. It helps to rediscover And to appreciate there own beauty, permitting at the own personality Of express yourself freely.

Mulla Mulla - useful to check the situations characterized by excess heat, such as, for example, sweats, symptoms from the syndrome pre- menstruation, vaginitis, flushes of heat in menopause.

Old Man Banksia - gives the ability to handle any challenging situation that life presents. Rebalance the activity thyroid.

Peach Flowered Tea tree - specific for the moods swinging; rebalances, on plan physicist, the activitypancreatic.

Pink Flannel Flower - offers the opportunity Of appreciate and enjoy everything, even the little things that life brings reserve.

She oak - it helps to exceed the imbalances hormonal in any phase from the life Of a woman, favoring the rebalancing of ovarian activity. Specific remedy for the rebalancing of the ovaries.

Supplement with seven drops under the tongue, morning and evening. Massage gently on zones you wish morning And evening. Vaporize frequently in the environment frequented.

Fluent Expression

Free your voice, giving courage and clarity in facing any situation that requires good verbal fluency e vocal. Favors the expressiveness And the find from the creativity. They come mixed together:

Bush Fuchsia - favors there communication interhemispheric cerebral, attenuating those difficulty of learning and expression that often derive from a marked lateralization functional. This essence brings the sense of security needed to speak in public and to expose what you believe in, improving the stamp and the melody from the voice.

Crowea - attenuates the concerns associated to the speak in public or to attend performances. Has a strengthening, calming effect, centered on body and mind. Releases the tension accumulated in the bronchial muscles, allowing for proper breathing. It gives calm and equilibrium in expression Of emotions, also Of nature intense.

five Corners - increases love own And self-esteem. IS Of relief at problematic Of bad posture of the body, Of breathing And Of stuttering.

Flannel Flower - it helps to to enjoy of the sensations physical and in particular the sensitivity to physical contact with the other, resizing the own borders. Donate freedom in expressing if themselves garlic other.

Red Grevillea - weight scale the articulation tempore-mandibular, permitting a more efficient fluence verbal. Like this doing, there own independence And the own courage will emerge spontaneously And there yes will hear excessively conditioned come on ratings others.

Tall Mulla Mulla - promotes the feeling of being tall

completely relaxed and secure with others and encourage social interactions, eliminating the fear of confrontation. Improve breathing problems and energy blockages in the apparatus respiratory.

Turkey Bush - it helps the people to tune in And to express your creativity. Renew confidence in own capacity artistic.

To integrate with seven drops under there tongue, morning And evening.

oppression Free

Helps to break free from emotional blockages that cause feelings of heaviness mental and physical. Promotes the elimination of toxins by the mind and body. Particularly indicated in Association to programs draining And how Help in diets detoxifiers And slimming. They are mixed together:

Bauhinia - offers the possibility to become more flexible and more open to new realities, situations and ideas. It helps get rid of prejudices wrong.

Favors the balancing from the valve ileo cecal.
bottle brush - allows of to live there life And the its inevitable changes, intelligently overcoming the past and serenely waiting for new experiences of life. It helps to face up to with serenity the changes. Favors there colon detoxification.

Bush Iris - perception from the reality And from the spirituality to theOf there of the plan material And physicist. It helps the activity of the lymphatic system which is one of the major pathways of elimination of toxins from the body.

Dagger Hakea - helps the person express their own feelings openly And to forgive. Favors the elaboration and the consequent resolution of details situations full of resentment and hatred. Promotes the detoxification physics for the its activity on liver.

dog Rose - laugh trust And safety in self themselves. It helpsto discover a renewed courage to face others, fully embracing and enjoying the meaning of life. Favors the elimination from the fear, emotion closely related to the kidneys on which it has action draining.

wild Potato Bush - give a sense Of freedom And vitality to then regain the freedom to change. Help them people who perceive their body as if it were a obstacle, giving a sensation Of freedom.

To integrate with seven drops under there language, morning And evening.

Optimism

Removes negative patterns, loss and low trust future, allowing for a mental and emotional openness that allows Of to enjoy of abundance that the future has potentially in Serbian for everyone. Very useful for discouraged people, who tend to focus only on the negative aspects, with there trend to strengthen them talking about it continuously. They come mixed together:

bluebells - promotes there trust in abundance universal, a condition that give a cheer contagious. Useful for the children that not by hand to share the They games with the other.

Boab - it helps to to break free from those models mental and familiar emotions rigidly acquired and who are handed down from generation to generation. Delete those familiar opinions that may prejudice the possibility to get rich. Useful in experiences of abuse, persecution and prejudices.

Christmas Bell - helps to manifest one's wishes and needs, giving the opportunity to learn to appreciate both at to donate that to to receive.

Five Corners - gives self-esteem, helping to accept if themselves And to appreciate there own beauty inner. Increases self-esteem and vitality, so as to improve the own relations.

Philoteca - allows you to openly accept your own successes and the accolades that they derive from it.

Pink Flannel Flower - offers the opportunity Of appreciate and enjoy everything, even the little things that life brings reserve.
Promotes a sense of gratitude, happiness and joy for the life, permitting Of feel the events newspapers through a positive vision, in the awareness thatany event is in most cases usefulfor

the own evolution.

Southern Cross - encourage to to exploit the own potential and to create a positive vision of life. It helps people that they suffer Of self pity.

Sunshine Wattle - it helps to accept And to to enjoy there beauty of the present, having faith in the possibilities that offers the future, without being overly focused about the difficulties of the past. Promotes optimism and joyful expectations for the future.

To integrate with seven drops lot there tongue, morning And evening.

Physical Wellness

The Essence Combined Of Flowers Australians physical Wellness give Welfare physicist, acceptance, love And treatment physics of the own body. Improve acceptance, contact and awareness of your body by promoting self-massage. It helps to relate in a serene and balanced way with all the characteristics of own physicality.
They are mixed together:

Billy Goat Plum : complete and conscious acceptance of one's body, discovery or rediscovery of pleasure sexual.

Five Corners : love and self-acceptance. It helps rediscover and appreciate your own beauty, permitting at the own personality Of express yourself freely.

Flannel Flower : helps to enjoy the physical sensations and in particular the sensitivity to physical contact with the other, resizing the own borders. Donate freedom in expressing if themselves garlic other.

Little Flannel Flower : rediscovery of the desire to play And Of joke, Of to have fun, the everything under the sign from the spontaneity.

Mulla Mulla : Reduces the negative effects of fire and gods rays solar.

She Oak : helps to overcome fluctuations positively mood them in women.

Wisteria : gives confidence in yourself and in your partner. It helps to break up to go, permitting at own feelings of expressing yourself freely.
Relationships

Improve the quality of all interpersonal relationships, especially familiar ones; gives the ability to manage in a balanced way emotionally charged situations in both adults and children. Free from resentments, confusion and conditioning negatives family members, attenuating there suffering that often neither follows. Encourage there creation Of new relationships social.
They come mixed together:

Bluebell - opens the heart, restores joy and desire for emotional participation with the other

Boab - removes assimilated negative patterns and examples with the education receipt give her figures parenting or from other Of reference. It helps to not recreate possible conditions negative occurred in the own family.

bottle brush - allows Of to live there life And the its inevitable changes, intelligently overcoming the past and serenely waiting for new experiences of life. Promotes a healthy, mutual mother-to-child relationship son.

Bush Gardenia - renew the passion and interest in relations interpersonal, because gets better the skill Of communication and attention towards the other.

Dagger Hakea - it helps to externalize one's feelings openly And to learn to forgive. Favors the elaboration and the consequent resolution of details situations loads Of resentment and hatred.

Flannel fFower - it helps to to enjoy of the sensations physical and in particular the sensitivity to physical contact with the other, resizing their own borders.
Donate freedom in expressing self themselves garlic other.

Mint Bush - scales and smoothes moods, harmonizes the emotion. It helps to regain clarity, calm And skills in the manage also the situations Of character spiritual.

Red Helmet Orchid - fosters the bond between father and son, arriving at the rediscovered Of a renewed form of sensitivity And Of respect.

Red Suva Frangipani - it helps the people that they stand crossing a moment particularly difficult And tension load due to the loss of a loved one or the breakup of a relationship. Facilitates processing of the feelings associated with lost of love.

Wedding Bush - helps to engage in relationships, a ask yourself of the goals And to devote yourself at the They realization.

To integrate with seven drops under there tongue, morning And evening.

Self-confidence

It brings out the positive effects of self-esteem and self-confidence themselves. Allows Of feel to own comfortable in half to other people and resolves the negative opinion about them in a constructive way own capacity And the senses of past guilt.
It gives awareness of one's abilities and power, not just of change events, but also to act coherently with oneself themselves. They come mixed together:

Boab - Free your mind from familiar conditioning acquired rigidly. Tone down those opinions that they limit the individual mentally and emotional And that I am invariably acquired And handed down Of generation in generation.

dog Rose - laugh trust And safety in self themselves. It helpsto discover a renewed courage to face others, embracing And enjoying completely of the sense from the life.

five Corners - it helps to accept each other appreciating there beauty in all its facets. It is a suitable essence in case of low self-esteem, lack of confidence with if themselves and of lack of self love.

Southern Cross - encourage to to exploit the own potential and the creation of a positive vision of life.
It helps to open up to the idea of a life full of opportunities living in the round, promoting the elimination of self-victimhood.

Sturt Desert Rose - allows Of follow the own beliefs more deep And there own morality And Of find one renewed integrity personal. Restore the level Of self esteem that suffers a lowering to cause of the senses Of guilt.
To integrate with seven drops under there tongue, morning And evening.

Sexuality

Combination of Floral Essences suitable for both men and women the woman, who helps to eliminate shame and shyness. It allows the person to accept himself completely and feel at ease comfortable with your body, learning to let go to physical intimacy. Renew passion and interest in the relationship amorous.
They come mixed together:

Billy goat Plum - is mainly specific for the feelings of aversion or revulsion towards oneself, especially when they are addressed to organs or acts sexual. Also useful for skin problems, such as acne, eczema, psoriasis, herpes, warts that they compete tocause a sensation Of body "not clean".

Bush Gardenia - renew the interest towards the other, getting better there communication interpersonal. It helps the partners to regain interest in each other, avoiding taking for granted and coming back to express interest for the mate with renewed vitality. Favors the finding a new complicity. Rediscovery of passion.

Flannel Flower - it helps to to enjoy of the sensations physical and in particular the sensitivity to physical contact with the other, resizing the own borders. Donate freedom in expressing if themselves.

Fringet Violet - removes the negative consequences of worry for the here I'm And for the past, protecting the integrity of the psyche. Specific in the cases of abuse sexual for the overcoming of the shock also through there sensation Of greatest safety And stability.

Little Flannel Flower - rediscovery of the desire to play And Of joke, Of to have fun... the everything under the sign from the spontaneity.

Sturt Desert Rose - allows Of follow the own beliefs more deep And there own morality And Of find a renewed personal integrity by eliminating the sense of guilt.

Wisteria - gives confidence in yourself and your partner, satisfaction and pleasure in the activity sexual.
It helps to break up to go, permitting at own feelings of expressing yourself freely.

To integrate with seven drops under there tongue, morning And evening.

Solaris

It represents an essential remedy in giving relief after a burns from fire or prolonged exposure to the sun. It's a combination excellent for to help to calm the ache or the tied burning to all the types of sunburn.
Of great help to people who can't stand the heat. Reduces significantly there quantity Of radiation absorbed from theSun, come on rays x And from the radio therapy. Useful also in case Offlushes of heat during there menopause.
They come mixed together:

Mulla Mulla - removes the memories physical And psychological symptoms of burns of any kind (water boiling, hot objects, sun). Helps prevent side effects negatives due to a excessive exposure solar. Promotes the elimination of fear related to fire and negative effects of radiation stored in the body. The recruitment Of this essence, after some day, it could lead to the appearance of some marks on the body reminiscent of those experienced during sunburn. Taken first Of a long flight airplane protects give her waves electrostatic.

She oak - in following to a sunburn promotes an action rehydrating, giving elasticity to skin.

Spinifex - helps in case of blisters or rashes due to excessive exposure solar or to sunburn.

To integrate with seven drops under there language, morning And evening. To integrate, Moreover, with seven drops right away after the episode.

Spirituality

It awakens spirituality, because it leads to deepening the practice religious or spiritual. Gets better access to the ego more evolved while simultaneously providing for the protection of the psyche e to integrity of the Aura that wraps it. Particularly indicated towho practices meditation. They are mixed together:

Angelsword - favors there rediscovered of the values of the past, the rediscovery of spiritual Truth, of Peace interior and renews communication with our Self more deep.

Boronia - promotes clarity Of thought And serenity mental. Helps to increase the ability to maintain intense concentration during there meditation.

Bush Fuchsia - favors there Jack Of consciousness of the own intuitions, to finally be able to listen to them and for to feed trust in they. Brings to a balancing between the hemisphere logical rational And the hemisphere creative And intuitive, that is respectively the left And the right.

Bush Iris - allows to the individual Of log into at the own spiritual dimension and to open the doors of own perceptions more in time. Allows that there faith you penetrate into deep within the individual.

Fringet Violet - removes the negative consequences of worry for the here I'm And for the past, protecting integrity from the psyche.

Green Spiders Orchid - favors the expression Of potential extra-sensory abilities. Allows you to enter harmony with all living beings and with one dimension metaphysics. It helps spiritual teachers to transmit the own knowledge to the Of beyond the words.

Red Lily - helps to discover and mature concreteness and there concentration on what's this And to learn to to live thehere I'm. Stimulate engagement spiritual.

To integrate with 7 drops under there language, morning And evening.

Stress Stop

It helps counter the States anxious, favors the relaxation, attenuates the inconvenience physical caused give it stress. Harmonize the rhythms biological and improving the quality of sleep in adults and in children allows Of to reach the relaxation necessary for a good restful sleep. Lets learn how to delegate tasks, to devote time and space to yourself without letting go overwhelm from agitation and concern.
They come mixed together:

Black Eyes Susan - helps slow those paces down sometimes pressing And to reconsider there own interiority, discovering the center from the quiet in self themselves. Donate the opportunity to learn how to delegate tasks when these are excessive. Also useful for people who they eat very quickly, swallowing food with voracity And that can Of consequence manifest digestive problems.

bottle brush - allows Of to live there life And the its inevitable changes, intelligently overcoming the past and waiting serenely the new experiences of life. Very useful for "programmer" people that they suffer excessively the changes Ofplan.

Boronia - promotes serenity and clarity of thought, mostly when the stress assumes shapes obsessive. Tone down the thoughts nagging And unpleasant, helping to stop the brooding that often they competeto the emergence of insomnia.

Bush Fuchsia - promotes the finding of harmony, from the capacity Of I listen And from the trust in owninsights. Favoring a more efficient communication
Inter hemispheric cerebral, gets better there concentration And attention.

Crowea - has a remarkable effect calming And invigorating for body and mind, giving an intense sense of well-being and peace.

It is a great remedy for anxiety that it can cause muscle contractures and has a very good effect balancing on stomach getting better the related digestive problems to stress.

Jacaranda - remedy elective for one state Of over-excitement. It gives balance, decision and clarity of thought, advocating the creation of precise strategies and effective tools that allow you to complete each project with success.

Little Flannel Flower - Very useful for the people particularly busy that they tend to to live there daily life with excessive seriousness And rigidity.

Paw Paw - strengthens the intuitive process, so as to make more' accessible the solutions to the problems. When yes is in the position of having to make important decisions, loosen the impression Of excessive responsibility on selfthemselves.

Supplement with seven drops under the tongue, morning and evening. Massage gently on body And more specifically on zones where is it they tend to manifest inconvenience physical, how contracturesmuscle caused give it stress. Vaporize often in environmentswhere they are living tensions and nervousness.

Transition

Combination useful for whoever stay coping big changes organic or Of situations Of life, how a moving house, a change of nationality, a new job, a pregnancy, the menopause. Gives the ability to be open to change and to to be ready at challenges that they entail.
It also helps to remove the fear of death, giving calm and calm during the ride in the afterlife.
They come mixed together:

Autumn leaves - favors the ride from the reality material to that spiritual, abandoning there fear of death when it is near, in awareness from the naturalness of this important transition.

Bauhinia - it helps in the cases in which you be resistance to the changes. Sign to to receive, understand And accept new ideas, situations and people.

Bottlebrush - helps to cope with life transitions, trusting in own skills to manage the new situations. Gives the ability to overcome feelings of oppression, inadequacy, uncertainty and apprehension in the moment of the change. It helps to overstep the past, to be able to serenely face the news that the life brings.

Bush Iris - relieves feelings of deep relative fear to death. It is of benefit to those people who think there is nothing after the death. This essence helps consider the possibility that there is a spiritual reality, beyond to that that the five senses humans they succeed to feel.

Lichen - acts when the combination transition he comes Jack first from the death, in how much
assists in the separation that is for future between body physical and body etheric.

Mint Bush - from clarity in the changes more important that

Of usual they bring at the confusion mentalgiven by the feeling
that little or nothing is solvable. These changes include divorce,
failures, diseases serious, accidents, ride from a religion to
another one.

Red Grevillea - helps to find the strength to leave at shoulders
situations unpleasant And to find the audacity in undertaking
finally there own Street. Makes indifferent to the ratings of the
other And independentpsychologically.

Silver Princess - specific to situations where you have the
feeling like you have no purpose in life. It helps find there
direction with renewed motivation Andawareness.

To integrate with seven drops under there tongue, morning And
evening.

Travel

It is of benefit to those suffering from worries and fears of facing any type of displacement. Helps deal with travel with power And serenity, favoring the sense practical And allowing you to enjoy of the advantages to it related.
They come mixed together:

Banksia Robur - favors the recovery of energy And from the vitality after the labors Of a trip.

Bottle Brush - allows of to live with serenity everyone the changes that there distance from home it involves, including the change in diet that may involve difficulty intestinal,

Bush Fuchsia - helps in cases of dizziness and malaise from travel and promotes recovery in related problems to the melted hours. Favors there communication inter hemispheric cerebral, attenuating those difficulty of learning and expression that often derive from a marked lateralization functional.

Bush Iris - favors the activity of the system lymphatic preventing the excessive swellings due at the static from the position during the travel. Rebalance there pineal gland and is therefore useful in problems tied to the jet lag.

Crowea - has a remarkable effect calming And invigorating on body and mind, giving an intense meaning Of Welfare And quiet. IS a great remedy for anxiety.

Fringet Violet - removes the negative consequences of worry for the here I'm And for the past, protecting integrity from the psyche.

Macrocarpa - renew the enthusiasm, there vitality, the energy.

Mulla mulla - reduces the effects negatives of electromagnetism.

Paw Paw - stimulates the ability to deal with a problem with lucidity And clarity.

Red Lily - it helps to discover And to to mature there concreteness And concentration on things and learning to live the here I'm. Stimulate engagement spiritual.

She Oak - helps overcome hormonal imbalances in women. Relieves the symptoms Of dehydration that frequently yes they try during And immediately after a flight airplane And embankment the effects from the pressurization aerial on female hormones.

Silver Princess - finding direction and purpose purpose from to assign at the own life. Renewed motivation and awareness.

Sundew - brings out practical sense, attention to i details in the totality of things, concentration and the precision.

Tall Mulla Mulla - helps you feel comfortable and confident in half to other people. Encourage the relations social.

Supplement with seven drops under the tongue, morning and evening. Massage on zones subjects to swellings And dehydration during the travel.